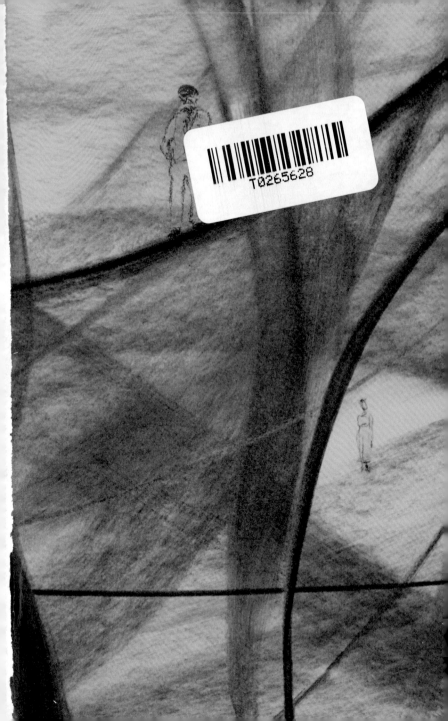

Praise for *Entanglements*

Turning away from the noise of straightforward confession, Leah Souffrant chooses instead the murmuring intertext, the silent and slow route of listening to the shudder of language at those sonorous points where suffering and rapture collide and then part ways. Studying *Entanglements* entangles me in Souffrant's open-hearted archive, and renews my faith in the poetics of bibliomancy, that charmed zone where yearning and reading intersect, and where Souffrant, terse as Duras, shows us how to feel at home.

Wayne Koestenbaum

The force of Leah Souffrant's roving, probing mind and the remarkable distances it both maps and collapses is exquisite. In this inspiriting, genre-refuting work, we encounter life's difficult enmeshings, richly braided together with critical acuity, care, and verve. Souffrant's vision, and what it alights on, is sui generis.

Jenny Xie

A capacious, loving textile where meditations become fibers through which questions about art, memory, love, and human relationships intertwine, Leah Souffrant's *Entanglements* will change how you think about reading, texts and bodily encounters with the world. *Entanglements* pulls at the fibers of history and humanity, inviting the reader to think about new ways of touching life and its artifacts. Simply put, this is a gorgeous book—and the reader will, too, become entangled in its brilliance and artistry and emerge changed.

Tyler Mills

Love, memory, meaning, nation, narrative — with *Entanglements*
Leah Souffrant touches every thread of the web, causing vibrations
that remind us of how we are bound to the world and one another.
That frisson, of coming into contact with the invisible, might once
have been evidence of witchcraft, but now it is how we recognize
poetry of colossal proportions. To look so unflinchingly at the invisible
web that holds everything together, to feel its umbilical tug on your
own life, requires a form of courage that Souffrant has in spades and,
with her writing, she'll lend you some.

Abby Paige

Entanglements is a true "text" in the etymological traces of the word:
both the act of weaving and the object woven. Leah Souffrant braids
the philosophical, lyrical, bodily, gestural — historical memory and
the memory of skin and sensation — in this mobile interface of
transitions. In its vibrating incantations, Souffrant's multimodal
Entanglements rims generic borders ... with indulgent thoughtfulness
and disarming intimacy.

Chris Campanioni

Entanglements

Threads woven from history, memory, and the body

Entanglements Leah Souffrant

UNBOUND EDITION PRESS

Atlanta

FIRST EDITION

Printed in the United States of America

LIBRARY OF CONGRESS RECORD

Name: Souffrant, Leah, 1975– author.
Title: Entanglements: Threads woven from history, memory, and the body / Leah Souffrant.
Edition: First edition.
Published: Atlanta : Unbound Edition Press, 2023.

LCCN: 2022951808
LCCN Permalink: https://lccn.loc.gov/2022951808
ISBN: 979-8-9870199-1-7 (softcover)

Designed by Eleanor Safe and Joseph Floresca
Printed by Bookmobile, Minneapolis, MN
Distributed by Itasca Books

123456789

Unbound Edition Press
1270 Caroline Street, Suite D120
Box 448
Atlanta, GA 30307

*The Unbound Edition Press logo and name are
registered trademarks of Unbound Edition LLC.*

PERMANENT

Contents

Introduction: Entanglements: poetic epistemology

> Whoever cannot seek
> the unforeseen sees nothing,
> for the known way
> is an impasse.
>
> > Heraclitus, trans. B. Haxton

> How does it all begin? I suppose it never begins. It just
> continues.
>
> > Martha Graham

If I dwell on these words in an airport, in an airport at a table writing, in an airport awaiting a flight and at a table next to a man talking to another in a lilting accent, then I write this entangled with that, with these observations. Where are you reading? What do you see and feel?

The work of these entanglements is to acknowledge not the problem of explanation but its impossibility, at least in any complete sense.

Entangled.

Explaining, where to explain is to delimit, is here entangled with an expansive poetics, a poetics of non-delimiting. My poetics recognizes the arbitrariness of limits, yet marks them anyway — for style, for rhythm, for pattern. When it comes to knowing, the poetic also knows the ironic. I am asking: How can we show the ways we know — or might project into knowing — while still acknowledging how knowledge fractures, bends, disperses, disobeys? Nodding towards the disobedience, a movement of the whole head. I answer how: the showing must become lyric.

What are the men in the airport talking about? The terminal air suddenly becomes fragrant with food. The fragrance changes the writing. I write with a hunger, but a tender kind of hunger. The flight will come in a few hours, and meanwhile I will eat. What has this to do with knowledge?

Nothing I explain is outside this writing, and as I explain it transforms in the telling. But there are countless pieces entangled, unknown, taking shape and changing the work. The travel that might take place. The arrivals of passengers full of excitement. And passengers slow with exhaustion, bored with business. The man next to me asks his interlocutor, "Have you been to the Austin airport?" Which terminal do you see me in? How terminal could any terminal be, how otherwise than yours? I have not been to Austin, I think silently. Where have we never been? Where are we not going, shaping the ideas?

In photographs documenting the now-abandoned airport in Athens, Greece, I see broken waiting areas, thousands of ticket stubs strewn on floors, stiff gray air. Seeing these photos of Europe, I think of the airport in Port-au-Prince, Haiti, which is not abandoned. It is an airport where I have been. What ghosts were there, in its crowding walls, its stiff Caribbean air? So many travelers' stories, like so many ticket stubs in the hand, then in the trash, now invisible in my imagination. How far is the Mediterranean from the Caribbean in this moment? The rhythms are more than linguistic.

I need poetic form to convey the ways we come to know and create the world we inhabit and experience, both as experience and through experience. These ways are necessarily multiple, plural. Hungry from the fragrances.

The poetic is not the rhythm of words, but the rhythm of experience — sometimes of words themselves — that becomes the world as we perceive it. This kind of knowing, a fragmentary wisdom, is often in tension with logic. The best scientists wonder more at the limitations of knowledge than its achievement — or achievability. Physics increasingly echoes the poetics of creative perception. Sometimes we hear uncertainty. Sometimes we hear entanglement. Sometimes both.

And still hungry.

Poetic knowing has long understood our limitations, the relativism of knowledge, the ways in which attention to what happens — its repetition, its patterns, its disruption — is how we come to understand anything, perhaps everything. And this arrival comes through the senses: sound, body, living even as we think. Some poets are trapped in history, poets seeing some humans and not others, loving only what might have been before them as love-worthy. Language has oppressed, imprisoned, ruined. Loosening chains requires a heat, fine, burning. Yet even these poets might have seen nonetheless a world created in our perceptions. Even here, a fragment of wisdom more capacious than law.

It's hard to discuss through traditional argumentation the ways in which argument and historical ways of affirming knowledge have been oppressive. How do we name how hard it is to know? The slow emergence of a mathematical proof without error, luminous, the slow layering of paint on a canvas that dries wild, true, luminous. The sudden inspiration. The graceful movement.

Imagine alternatives to argument. Practice new ways to understand or learn or show what we are in the process of knowing. Foreground questions instead of impossible answers. You don't know everything, but your experiences guide us away from this terror if we pay enough attention. Pay attention to the complexity of the threads that might mystify us, approach ease as you find more and more of what we offer each other, in each encounter with words and ideas and images and objects and each other.

Obviously, whatever we've been doing is not really working.

Just last week I was shown a rendering of the brain of a dolphin, and I feel utterly changed by it. The folds, so many, so dense, are more folds than in the rendering of the human brain, which appeared next to the image. The pattern I saw in the dolphin brain is more intricate, its elegance a tight, delicate weave. I look at the vivid depictions in nauseating pink and flat beige, drawings that can't reveal the secrets folded so densely behind a living dolphin's cool, round eyes. I look, but I will never be in any intimate way of knowing the dolphin, nor of understanding its brain. I am more poet than biologist, more artist than technician. Yet this brain is now with me. Just last week, I am changed. And you, too, having read this.

Forgo the protections of since it-has-been-so. What if it might be otherwise?

It is otherwise. We do love one another, without argument.

Thread: *And keep me all this night*

> Everyone has a captivity narrative; today we call it memoir.
> Stacy Schiff, *The Witches*

The answers we do not question draw us into a kind of captivity.

We are held captive, too, by the narratives. We feel for the sense of
a thread between question and answer, as if logic is real. We create
stories. The threads twist into a rope. Twists as rope around flesh.

○ ○ ○

Salem is a story. It's also the place where, family legend has it, the
records of some of my own ancestors are found. In *The Witches,*
Stacy Schiff posits, "Salem is in part the story of what happens
when a set of unanswerable questions meets a set of unquestioned
answers."Legends beget questions, fears become stories, stories shape
dreaded answers.

Visiting Massachusetts, I buy little reproductions of old books in gift
shops at various historic sites. They are made of flimsy paper, staple-
bound, sold in little plastic sleeves for a few dollars. Weeks later, I
write a poem.

1777 Primer

The New England Primer echoes
in the word fear. Learn the letter
A: *In Adam's Fall* / the children taught
some dark secret we carry.
We sinned all. And the secret is
la-den, dif-fi-cult, shared. It is our
meetinghouse. *Forgive me whatever*
I have done amiss this day/
Secrets, prayer *and keep me*
in secret, divinity in secret, *all this night*
fear of god that is the goal
of the Good, such is the alphabet *in sleep*
for generations. The f curls on the pages
like a hissing s. *While youth do chear/*
Death may be near. Born near
Salem, how did I hear the alphabet?
What is this thing they call
cell memory? *My Book*
and Heart/Must never part.

o o o

After she reveals that unanswerable questions meet answers that
aren't questioned, Schiff observes that the powers of women, the
legends of those powers, are given respect when they surprise us.

The powers of women are mysterious. Mystery takes away agency, replacing real impact with imaginary forces. When her powers come out of crises, they are accidental and thus wondrous — the strength begotten through miracle. Women's power, then, is denuded of its own power.

Power stripped, questions unasked, legends of crisis form legacies of impact.

o o o

The twists get knotted, just at the most tender places: the neck, here is the noose.

o o o

The souvenir we take from the museum is here to remind us of our visit, to conjure memories. The memory of the visit to a historic site has the double conjuring of a memory of a visit and a memory of a history, of which we may have learned only at some remove. I've been here before, in fact and otherwise.

There are many things — real locks, real metal bars, real strong arms holding us down. And the reasons claiming they can, or they ought. This too might astonish us, as do the deaths of those accused of witchcraft. Might we ask what answers fix the arms in place?

○ ○ ○

Weeks pass. I am busy with days. Interrupted by accumulating tasks: respond to queries, prepare for tomorrow, prepare for today, care for others, care for self, meet deadlines. When to dwell on an idea? Later, later.

This is the way we lose the patience for sorting through, for tracing the tangling thoughts, more than thoughts, the problem, one assumption, one misstep builds on another. The accountant ignores me, asks not a single question. There's a man in the room, the accountant asks him many questions. Answers are given.

I have some finances. Money is a kind of power, we all know. I offer some information. My finances are under consideration. I have some experience in these matters. My words drift into space, unheeded by the accountant. The accountant files the tax report, my information left out.

○ ○ ○

It takes patience to track the threads entangling.

○ ○ ○

In the museum hang enormous knotted ropes of fabric, from the ceiling two stories high, to the ground at my feet. A forest of these long fabric forms hang, with knots interrupting their draping. Poet and artist

Cecilia Vicuña created this "Disappeared Quipu" echoing an Andean tradition on a massive scale. The museum tells me, "For millennia, ancient peoples of the Andes created quipus — complex record-keeping devices, made of knotted cords, that served as an essential medium for reading and writing, registering and remembering."

o o o

The philosopher reads the other philosophers in *Slow Philosophy* and observes, "Patience involves exposing and subjecting myself to the other; coming near, in order that a relation be established, and the work of ethics done." She wants a slow philosophy to understand a deliberate ethics and reminds the reader, the slow reader, to be patient, but patience, too, is required to slow down.

o o o

"Salem is in part the story of what happens when a set of unanswerable questions meets a set of unquestioned answers."

o o o

The secret is laden, difficult. It could become our meetinghouse.

o o o

It takes a slow kind of thinking to mark the reach beyond the table, the room, outside the quiet of the accountant's head where my words are not heard, my information deflecting like a hand touching a too-hot surface. My words pop like blown bubbles hitting the lawn: some slowly, some instantly. The other man in the room with me is John, and he listens. He follows my words. Some go far, upward.

o o o

It takes patience to work through the connection between this conversation and Abigail Adams and words that reverberate for centuries. Don't forget the ladies, she implored in 1776. Pop pop. And we make the world out of things perceived. Pop. Perceiving. Pop pop. Or not perceiving.

o o o

Lovingly, we decide we won't return to this accountant. Lovingly, patiently, follow the thread.

o o o

In the museum, there are several ancient quipus in cases in the gallery around the large, sculptural creation by Vicuña. These knotted strings appear frail, worn. They are mysterious, yet recognizably formed. They are over half a millennium old. Placed carefully in the boxes, we might practice math to think back. How many lives have passed? How many hands must these have passed through, from their making to this careful preservation?

o o o

For a long time, when it suited them, the men turned to explanations
they called otherworldly. Bridget and Sarah and Elizabeth and
Susannah and Rebecca were all executed for witchcraft in 1692. Also,
another Sarah and George and John and Elizabeth's husband, another
John, another George. Alice and Mary and Wilmot and Ann. All
accused of witchcraft and executed by the state. Also, Margaret and
Martha, and another Mary from a nearby town. And Giles, who took
three days to die.

o o o

Foreshadowing Recalled

Turning up a bend in the road, under lush
        dark branches, a twilight hanging beyond
            them, boys cycled by squealing, rowdy.
                It's that walk, those black paved streets remembered,
while all the words are forgotten.

The secret is for you to forget, wrote Ritsos in a Greek prison.
    And life
            is full of prisons, if you look back, if you are naming things,
                if you locate memory by all the things it
                    could not touch. Cannot.

The air at twilight is warm yet comfortable. The dark
lets you see — pinks glowing orange, greens turning black,
birds startling the viscous trees when the wheels
swerve, too close, buoyant with violence — and see the
approaching obscurity. He wanted to keep walking. You wanted
to go home. But home disappeared with the light.

o o o

For a long time, when it suited me, I turned to spirit guides. I tossed
coins to make sense of the dissolution of a relationship. I turned
to coins with the fear of having been trapped without my own
awareness. Could my vague sense of captivity be explained by cards,
by coins, by lines drawn in skin or in the tea leaves, only just stirred?

Niels Bohr begins his collection on *Atomic Physics and Human
Knowledge* with this disclaimer: "The gist of the argument is that
for objective description and harmonious comprehension it is
necessary in almost every field of knowledge to pay attention to the
circumstances under which evidence is obtained."

It is an elegant elision to draw together objectivity and description,
and then harmony and comprehension. Harmonious comprehension
we might come to, but under what circumstances? What of the broken
heart? What of the oppressed spirit? What of the imprisoned body?

o o o

Home is often disappearing. Poet Yiannis Ritsos was held under
house arrest. Ritsos was exiled. Prison is more than a building. Secrets
are more than what we think we know.

○ ○ ○

Not evil, maybe, not the spirit (I almost remember the echoing
menace of *the serpent beguiled me*) but echoes and the task of
attention is to hear them (or *what serpent?*), to hear the echoes
on deeper and multiple registers. Rather than to shape them. But
the echoes may, they must be a music too, else whence the songs?
Fatalistic, this history is steeping in the rooted past, but we are fated
to turn over something impossible to know. Fated to secrets we aren't
aware we are keeping.

○ ○ ○

As late as the early 2000s, the Metropolitan Museum of Art included
on its correspondence lists of patrons that included the equivalent of
"Mrs. John Doe." Her name becomes a kind of sacrifice.

○ ○ ○

If superstitions are controlled, if fortunetelling is forbidden, one
might consider why. Control for what results? Against what risk?
Who is weakened by the 17th century reading of an egg's marks on
a glass? The people told mysteries through fortunetelling five years

ago on Madison Avenue and centuries ago in Salem. The people read mysteries in the egg's marks in Salem. Who loses control when I ponder the possibility of alternatives? The Greek women read the marks left by coffee on the bottom of the cups. Last year, last decade, last century. If the book sets rules, which must be obeyed, who writes it? Who reads it aloud? Who tells us not to ponder the potential of a twist of fate, a way of seeing outside the language given — given then re-given then served then restrained?

○ ○ ○

Of man's first disobedience and the fruit of that forbidden tree whose mortal fruit brought death into the world and all our woe — I have memorized these lines of Milton with such ease.

What is this thing they call cell memory?

One man in Salem was sentenced to death by heavy stones.

○ ○ ○

The hand can be read. Its lines tell a story. A palm open can tell you a single word: alternatives. Or: possibilities. Or: unknown. It might be a sorcerer. It might be a scam. It might be a high-five. A loving mother reaching to cradle the child's small round scalp.

One palm reminds us the book is but a holder of lines, bent and breaking, bendable and breakable.

○ ○ ○

The crisis in 1692 began with two girls having fits in the house of Samuel Parris, the minister of Salem Village. Now Danvers, Massachusetts.

My own birthplace is not far. Just drive south a few miles from Salem Village.

○ ○ ○

"It's the most dramatic instance of women's impact on the public realm before the 19th century in America and before the rise of the women's rights movement." Mary Beth Norton describes the trials and the executions in a lecture entitled "In the Devil's Snare: The Salem Witchcraft Crisis of 1692." This impact may have been dramatic, but rights are slow in coming. Outrage and whispers and justifications and alienation continue to swirl around discussions of "women's impact."

Almost 300 years after the trials in Salem, another girl complained after attacks from a man in Danvers. The spread of the complaints was limited. A private affair. A family matter. My grandfather sentenced merely to ostracism. The rest of us retreated into silence.

Only in hindsight I recognize the bravery of my own girlhood testimony.

○ ○ ○

Essex County was on the front lines of the Indian Wars at the time of
the trials in Salem Village. And the colonists were not winning. The
judges, whom we might imagine as stiff pious statesmen or religious
figures, were also military fighters in these wars. There is no neat
category for the judge. Nor the judged. Bravery becomes blame and
bravery again.

○ ○ ○

In the "new world" and the old, "Obedience was not only a religious
duty but a legal requirement." Take away rights, take away property,
take away name. The contract is not one of exchange, but of claim.
Remember the law of coverture, described by Blackstone in England
in 1765 and understood as the law of the land before and after that
date. In marriage, woman's very existence alters, hangs by a thread.
Even upon her husband's death, the court would determine who takes
hold of her pots and pans. Who takes hold of her children. By a thread,
her world. By a thread, her being.

Who is Mrs. John Doe?

It is hard to imagine coverture as anything other than terrifying.
What protection is this precarity? Blackstone's words creep into my

reading again and again: it is "under [the husband's] wing, protection, and cover, she performs every thing." This heavy cloak, this dark cloud. Rebecca Solnit writes neatly about wives' erasure: "She had no separate existence." Imagine, doing everything under, and especially in a social order where the highest values are — just that — high, beyond the reach of the protective layer above you. Kept covered, kept in the care, the "protection" is the very thing that prevents ascension. Whose protection is this, then, but those who control all this that becomes under it, under him. This obviousness of its stifling burden is staggering.

o   o   o

Things that are obvious, staggeringly so, are not necessarily changing or simple.

Yet, and in hindsight, too, I notice the woman listening. My mother, catching my words, understanding.

o   o   o

There may be no neat category for the judge or the judged. What is a witch anyway? What is a family? What is a private matter and what is a law enforced? Whose laws do I live by? What does it matter when betrayal's meaning is decided only by some, by power, and my power may only be available by miracle?

○ ○ ○

Eager to shed the false name of my own terrible paternal grandfather,
I happily grabbed a new one in marriage. Buoyant, my new signature
whispered "suffering" and is shared with a daughter, onward,
entangling me with expanding yet unknown possible networks. The
enslaved, the liberated, the cycling and naming the violence it does
name: suffering. The world multiplies with a name and the name's
insignificance also amplified — flung into oblivion, grabbed from
opportunity. I am, yet, in and out of the net. Covered and uncovered.
More importantly, discovering.

Those who investigate history pursue something that is at once the
discovery of insight, new sources, something that happened that
might reveal this past, and at the same time the relentlessness of
the past's undiscoverability, the inaccessibility of what is not now,
not immediate.

We learn that the quipus were banned during the period of
colonization by the Spanish in 1583. The knots were a language, and
the language became dangerous to colonizers. Lost in this silence may
be more than words.

"The woman who is represented is obscured, but the woman who
represents is not," Solnit observes. And we retrain our attention.

○ ○ ○

A poem provides some comfort. We turn to words for this language that will serve us differently than talk. The difference is in the poem's willingness to forgo insisting on its meaning, its knowing, its authority. The poem suggests instead of insists, exposing through gesture rather than explication. Through this relinquishing of authority, in various ways, through its various devices, sweeps, metaphors, music, murmurs, poetry asserts a mastery. Unsteady, open, ominous is this mastery. Poetry reveals, but what it reveals is never quite, never fully.

○ ○ ○

The poet might ask if what is immediate is accessible either. So fleeting is our grounding in this immediacy — as art reveals over and over, hand to hand. Fixing knowledge is a fool's errand, while also a necessary and satisfying pursuit.

Thread: *Attention to Loving*

> If I speak of Nature, it's not because I know what it is
> But because I love it, and for that very reason,
> Because those who love never know what they love
> Or why they love, or what love is.

Fernando Pessoa, "The Keeper of Sheep"

Some love finds you in passion. Skin feeds some spark. Some energy fills as thought.

Sometimes I'm so generous. I want the world to look kindly on that fire. I want the world to look kindly on the body all mixed up with idea, on past, on future, on you.

Sometimes I recognize you. Look at your body. As if listening, see your face, stare at your hands.

Some intensity of recognition tries to measure this strange and common insistence on seeing, watching, noticing, and attending — to you. Sometimes.

I want to fit the broken pieces together. Skin and eyes and ideas, memory and the touch, the touch now and its memory later.

o o o

I remember sitting on a bench in the spring sun, talking. Love in passion as the moment of touch and its before and its after, anticipation and recollection. I remember sitting on that particular bench and I remember a touch that never happened but might have. I'm alive in expectation, hopeful, then I'm alive in disappointment. I have felt disappointments so passionate that they felt like love. They were love.

○ ○ ○

After seeing a friend from the past, long estranged, I had a dream in which she offered me shards of stone on which were carved pictures, shapes of sea life, a broken story. She insisted I fit the shards together, and I took them, willing, curious, and began to hold the pieces. But it became clear that the broken shards could not fit into a cohesive whole, the story the fish told could not be completed, and the estranged friend in the dream was setting me an impossible task like some dancing bear. In the dream, a different friend intervened, posed a question, saved me, interfered by loving.

A different friend, one far off but never estranged, intervened with loving.

If I am able to compose this book, as I envision it, it will be an act of love. Some need unasked for to be filled, with generosity. *You know you don't have to do this.* I do it anyway. I want to fit together the shards. I know they will not make a story.

○ ○ ○

Kierkegaard begins *Works of Love* with the plain observation that
"If it were true — as conceited shrewdness, proud of being deceived,
thinks — that one should believe nothing which he cannot see by
means of his physical eye, then first and foremost one ought to give up
believing in love." This belief in seeing too is a deception, Kierkegaard
is quick to point out, and the pride of not being deceived is the
foolishness of a deeper deception. "Indeed, one can be deceived in
many ways; one can be deceived in believing what is untrue, but on
the other hand, one is also deceived in not believing what is true."
The hope, even the staunch belief, that love needs to be proven with
those *physical eyes* leads the conceited, proud person not to a greater
understanding or a surer footing in what can or should be believed —
and here we might say *believed in* — but rather worse deception. His
words are strong here: "To cheat oneself of love is the most terrible
deception; it is an eternal loss for which there is no reparation, either
in time or in eternity." The most terrible deception. We con ourselves
out of love.

○ ○ ○

Attention to love is a loving attention. Attention to what we may
not see.

We hesitate, we almost, we might say I love you and this hesitation
reveals our attention to love. Love's uncertainty awakens hesitation,

the slow attention, and what is altered by the attention we give it is love itself and our relation to love.

To say love is a generous speech, inviting. An invitation into understanding the uncertainty and attention to love, our relation to it together.

Imagine a wobbling and try to cradle it steady: this is "I love you." It's so necessary that we return to it, I keep saying love, keep hearing its song in different voices across the years. See the body of a newly matured singer cradling a dirty microphone on a stage or the voice of a long dead body recorded singing love, love. Always lilting into a question in the air or leaning into an unforeseen understanding, fleeting though it may be: love. Some attempt at loving moves the sound, and in the air, we almost see this act of loving.

Where does this tenderness come from? asks Marina Tsvetaeva.

The books insist it (*love!*) even as authors claim another title. Justice. Decay. War. Loss. Humor. We write about what we care about: love and how to make it or why we break it. The psychology and the survival and the how to and the look back. War War War. History and the future. What if and you must. The imagination and the fact, reaching for it. If only we could understand love, admit it.

What makes a difference?

o o o

I took the book first from the library shelf, lit under a yellow glow,
from a tall wooden shelf lined with green and red spines. Then, I took
it to the white-lit room. I spread it open on the glass, the copy machine
warm and ready. I spread the pages, pressed a palm over the woven
texture of the bare cover. I pushed the round button and watched the
glow slide slowly back and forth, glowing over the light of the words.
Откуда такая нежность?

The page spilled out of the machine, and I closed the book, buttoned
my jacket, walked to my room, my desk. With scissors I made a frame
around the stanzas, with tape I put them on the wall above my desk.
Откуда такая нежность? *Where does this tenderness come from?*

o o o

Love won't be the thing you expect. Expectation alters it. And all the
other threads are loosening and tightening.

o o o

I read the description of the nun who informs the mother of the
stillborn baby's cremation. In Marguerite Duras's *Wartime Writings*
she repeatedly tells me that they burn the babies' bodies. It haunts her
notebooks. Burning bodies, babies. This is the work of the convent.
And miles away, the concentration camps. Human beings, alive and

moving their hands, their eyes, their bodies.

If we make the world out of the perception of it, we see the news, we learn of the burning bodies, but what do we perceive? What world are we making? We imagine, but others made that world in space and time, present. It is, yet our world too. We lean into the newspaper story. We click on the article on the screen. We must. What does this knowing tell us about love? What must we learn?

o o o

I was kissed in front of a flickering tv screen in the dark and forgot it. I only remember the size of the room, its lack of windows, its door ajar. Jason was murderous on the screen, so I closed my eyes. Everything was scary, and I blamed it on the movie.

o o o

There are countless poems about love, until you turn to poetry to express just right the love you feel, and it doesn't quite match any of the poems you find. Each poem a bit too precise, or obtuse, not precise enough.

Tasked to select the poem to read at a friend's wedding, I suddenly found that all the best love poems don't capture the sense you have of the couple's love, or the feeling of love you hope to convey, or it doesn't feel as "true" as your hopes for this love are to you. The poems

are so lofty as to feel unreal, far, not lived love at all. The poems
are not this couple clasping hands before the loving eyes of their
community. Not this eye a bit wet with fear and tenderness.

o o o

I still love my adolescent beloveds. We call it crush. The ten-year-old
boy in the photo, now dead before he turned 40. I keep strangely
grieving young Brian, and how he taught me love's power, simply by
existing in proximity. *I see you*, blurry by a picnic table on a school
field trip under tall pine trees near the other boys, not quite laughing.
Each of us may be loved, even if we don't notice the classmate
watching, the camera snapping.

o o o

Love may follow you like a mean ugly fiend, and you might say
you don't want that big feeling, its ominous whelming, its creeping,
your not knowing if it will save you from a surprise attack or be
the attacker. Sometimes it might leave you standing there on the
sidewalk, half stunned in near humiliation, a cracked brown leaf fallen
in your own mean ugly hair.

Some trying to attend well helps, trying to shape the ephemeral. Love
so slippery, it emerges in fits and starts, it can be recognizable one day
and disfigured the next, inconsistent even when persistent. Love may
find you.

But the brown leaves, they too have a curious fragility, an autumnal warmth, like pie and cinnamon almost, like a blanket. The leaf reminds you of the warm indoors, how you need it.

You keep walking, more ready.

○ ○ ○

On a different school field trip, the kids looked at hand-written questions posted on the wall of the museum. Written to the public, by young hands in new penmanship, the wall was filled with paper squares, each carrying a question. Some asked about alternative universes: "What if _____ had never been born?" (A corrupt/feared/ despised leader, fill in the blank.) Some narrowed the imagined worlds to a sharper focus: "What if _____ had not been elected?" The many speculative questions stood out for their repetition. The one my child liked best and called most different: "What if we all loved harder?"

What if we all loved harder?

○ ○ ○

The practice of attention is also a commitment to love, to its *sometimes*, as it reveals its changes.

The books call it unrequited love. I remember moments of looking and wondering. It was so nourishing, even in its lonely way. I understand love better as it flourished in anticipation and waned without a body to touch. Maybe this is what fans feel like, with their celebrity passions. I'm not sure; I've never loved a stranger like that. Yet if I never touched you, that love too is a different kind.

My tall slender friend once, or often, sighed wistfully, "I wish there was a pill so I wouldn't have to eat every day." A strange wish, to replace the pleasure of taste and touch and smell with a pill, a kind of nothingness.

Love is mine. We learn to love by loving. But not only love. Not only by loving.

○ ○ ○

You sit down to write the poem to the beloved person, and the edges fray in every direction. Too unruly, too spilling, too minute and sprawling at once, nourishing and exhausting. This moment can't be all love, this poem can't say love. Words fail again, sometimes, all the time, flailing in this saying too.

Your ears perk up to lyrics in the countless songs, love inflects pop songs and rock ballads, songs of loss and songs of desire and songs of joy, all love songs. Love me tender and rock me all night long and I can't live without loving you. Not every song, but everywhere you go its rhythms follow. You wonder how a new love song could be written,

yet more emerge every day, cracking open a new way into
the difficulty of saying it, love.

○ ○ ○

Loving the babies who did not survive,
And loving the museum security guard who smiles at your
child's curiosity.

○ ○ ○

We read of the terrors. Human beings can be terrifying. We recognize
the terror. In the news: "couple abuses child for years, city workers
find child." Is the story about the child dead or alive? What magnetic
force draws us to this story? To this life? What are we learning?
Where is love in this life?

○ ○ ○

If you don't notice my living, your love, I speculate, may sometimes be
weak. I understand.

○ ○ ○

I look up Brian's obituary. His parents grieve his loss, but say
nothing about his life, his work, his death. The obscurity is ominous.
Tenderness swells like a wave unexpectedly knocking me under at the

beach. Crushing. We know it's an ocean, but the push is a surprise.

○ ○ ○

The poem we seek but never find, the poem we need when
celebrating the friend's wedding. The proximity is not to the love we
recognize in art, but to that impossible-to-capture thing, that desire to
say what can't be said, not quite. The poem we want to give a tenderly
desired valentine, to admit some revelation, a new kind of knowing.
This poem will be ever revised, ever renewed, never achieved. I love
you is never really exhausted, unless love is extinguished — watered
down to ashes. The hollow ring renders it but mute.

○ ○ ○

Striving to learn the language, I read the poem over and over. такая
нежность. The tenderness of the stranger, from a distance, and
the strangely beautiful recognition of the stranger's own echoing
tenderness, "on the lips of the singer" was love to me, was love's
recognition, was the beauty of the unrequited and real. Tenderness.

We get songs in our head. We study poems. We read novels with plots
of loss and persistence and passion and betrayal. But love is not a plot.
It takes a long time to learn this. Always learning it.

○ ○ ○

As the pilgrims hover in the ship at the shore, in winter, William Bradford writes observations. Uncertain to land or turn back, more likely to perish than be preserved, but persisting, he writes, "Our fathers were Englishmen which came over this great ocean, and were ready to perish in this wilderness," seeing the shore dark, wild. Bradford is a pious man, a pilgrim, parsing out his love greedily. He observes in near exclamation his hope for the newly arriving pilgrims: "let them who have been redeemed of the Lord, show how he hath delivered them from the hand of the oppressor." Such limited possibilities for redemption, such hard vision. Pilgrims, oppressed, don't see the peoples they meet with loving vision. No tender view details this colonist's description.

There are different ways to cheat ourselves of love, as Kierkegaard feared, centuries and an ocean away. To love in increments, to love in fear, to be blind to love's possibilities is a kind of cheating too.

Arriving in that wilderness, afraid to love yet relying on faith and its loving ways, he said we find "no city to dwell in." Perhaps we cannot love what we do not perceive.

o o o

Where does this tenderness come from?
And what to do with it?
                                    Marina Tsvetaeva

o o o

Maybe unrequited love is like the hand spilling water it never could hold, but the mind stays damp with hope, with imagination. I need to imagine love, but can't imagine it without feeling it, too, the touch and taste. I don't want the pill.

Love and loss. Love and trauma. Love and emptiness. I wrote about it anyway. Try to crack open the pill and let the taste out. A kind of rebellion for the love we hold, we create, we swallow up.

o o o

The poet, too, returns to love, as if after every journey needing rest or hydration or just a bed to flop on. It's there in the angry words and the craving for justice. But though the writers have written love, the poet is haunted — by not only life's losses and kisses and desires, but language's echoes. "I love yous" barked and whispered, empty signatures at the bottom of Christmas cards, love. Emails, love you. Words, the poets remind us, still come, trying to get closer. Stop saying love, just do it, just don't, be in love, stop, look directly at the thing, the world, the space, language, oh sentimentality, as if knowledge were something and not another way into it, love.

o o o

You forget my birthday and it *breaks my heart*. Then I remind you, then you remember, and we learn it again.

○ ○ ○

Love thine neighbor as thyself — Simone Weil reminds us of the
book — saying it implies the inverse. If god loves us, we too might love
ourselves as divine creation. What might it change to imagine a loving
self as an act of faith in action? The supernatural, or what is beyond
the logic of known. What is love that extends its understanding of
meaning beyond the relation between me and you to a significance
outside the self and world but is made manifest in the self and
world? So, by doing well and right by all, we include our loving self,
not in selfishness, but in generosity of a world that doesn't pit each
against each but might see us all as a we or *entangled*. Entangled,
my love of each includes me, but this loving as action performs
without excluding the other, the others, indeed the other is not as
such distinguished from me. My joy and my joy for your happiness,
pleasure, and peace are inextricable too.

○ ○ ○

I sit in a café, editing a series of reflections on love and quietly
observing the people coming in and going out, sitting, working. Some
speak, others frown silently. Some work at the counter serving people
or wiping messes, taking cash. Others work in solitude, as I do, or
remotely through a screen. I sit and contemplate loving as a woman
leans forward to offer a small child a small bite of food.

○ ○ ○

Knowing the wilderness they encountered was not empty, we read Bradford's Mayflower papers and circle and recircle history, it begins and begins again. The awe of the persisting pilgrims exists, erupts in magnificence even as it simultaneously shrinks in its own blindness: to the humanity that greeted the ships. To be both wise and ignorant, beautiful and ugly, light with the spirit and heavy with the spiritual. I swell in the multiplicity of the history, but it doesn't get disentangled. Can I observe the bravery of the foot stepping off the Mayflower onto shore, recognize some hope for deliverance, even as I observe it ominously from the shadows, weapon held ready, or newborn held close?

o o o

Love won't be the thing you expect. In expectation, the threads, loosening and tightening. The shards line up with gaps.

o o o

The poets again with all that feeling, slowing us down. In your face with it, what is it, do you recognize it, the missing piece. A not quite retrieved memory tugged up the dark corner as the stairwell bent in your loving grandparents' home. The ache, the tender, the fierce, the said and unsaid again and again. The poets keep speaking uttering shaping it up and breaking it down and breaking it. Trying to get closer.

What if we all loved harder?

o o o

You bring home a birthday cake, moist with sweetness and butter.

o o o

In response to my sincere "I love you," in the home, unprompted
by anything but feeling, my child, to test values learned elsewhere,
responds, "I love you more," and looks expectantly for a response. *No*
is the only possible answer. It is not possible. Not possible to measure.
Not possible to claim. The child has been out in the world; this is
evidence of the corruption.

My answer pleases the child enough that the dialogue is repeated
until it becomes a game, a test for me to pass or fail every so often.
Each time, my saddened eyes intrigue the child a bit more until the
responses draw forth her explanations. "I know, I know, I get it. It's just
funny you know, I mean, how about an inch, how about a quarter of
an inch ... " A child's excuses for the mean joke of measuring love.

o o o

In the café, sometimes the child drops the food, and a passerby might
stop to pick it up. *Thank you* murmurs the mother, tired. Is the
contented child loving too? Isn't she?

Must be-loving mean be-loving-something or someone outside? Does love need an object and if so does its object matter? If we think of love in this, Weil's, sense — as a way of living in (relation to) a divine-thus-right way, then its object is less important than how loving alters how we interact. With love, we can't objectify or harm. Yet can we?

∘ ∘ ∘

The myth of family love, conflating family relation with loving, is often tragic. Relation by chance isn't love by default. How much violence? Broken promises, trust, how many broken bones in the family? The standard set by Weil is strict, high, daunting: evaluating love against divine love, imagining a human capacity for nearing, reaching toward the love we imagine possible of divinity. Yet in tenderness and generosity and devotion, there it is. This is not the love of family by default, but work, effort, and a kind of faith necessarily tested by living.

∘ ∘ ∘

Love won't be the thing you expect. Love won't be — what you expect love to be. What you expect of love. Expectation alters love.

Expectation might become impatient and corrupt love in its tightening, its rigidity, its leaning toward capture. And what you expect of love will not be found in the captive.

Knowing love changes love. Thinking love alters what you know of it.

○ ○ ○

A loving kiss, a trace of the hand reaching toward possible connections. The faces I have loved and touch and loved and not touched. There is love enough, love enough. *That which is has already been* (Eccl). So too is love entangled, yet my love today is also extraordinary and original. Love is not the who but the loving, and the commitment to making love, what Kierkegaard describes as duty. I will love, I shall love, ever better and more. This too, has already been, thus we might recognize it.

○ ○ ○

To look lovingly across the subway car, seated after a long day, and to see a person, and to see this person lovingly, it changes everything.

○ ○ ○

It is in loving, Kierkegaard tells us, that we become capable of love, able to love. Another conundrum, but lovely, loving, active. "[I]n loving you may eventually reach the point of loving the men you see," expresses the effort, what the philosopher-theologian calls "duty": to see, notice, attend, and respond to the people we encounter "loving" them, without seeking perfection, because this, in his theology, is God's expectation and creation.

It changes everything, even if the person does not look back.

Loving the man with the surprisingly bright shoes.

Loving the woman with the sad eyes.

Loving the person with the large yellow bags overstuffed with papers.

Loving the one with the torn shirt and broken shoes.

Loving the one asleep. The one talking loudly. The one who sees
you loving.

o o o

The very test of love is a proof of the definition's inadequacy. There
is no measure, the measure is a joke. Is not this the very antithesis of
every value that has claimed rank in the nation, in the capitol, in the
hierarchy that which by definition oppresses? To love would be to
imagine otherwise.

o o o

Life, liberty, love. A more radical demand for the American dream.

o o o

We talk about love beginning and ending. Love's falling into and out
of, as if it were a place, a pit, a hole into which we descend and ascend
from, as if to be out of love is a liberation or expulsion — release. But if
I am loving, I am loving. If I loved, I can find that love in me, I don't fall
out of it. Maybe I bury it, or it becomes overshadowed by other loves.
Or, when we "move on" by other feelings, maybe disappointment or

anger or frustration. These are all there too, entangled. But the love remains, if I loved.

Love becomes traceable if I loved you decades ago, if there was loving feeling, then it emerges when you emerge in my mind. This love is not dangerous, if I welcome love as a way of being.

I saw the woman with the yellow bags so many years ago. I remember her still.

Keep asking the question: Imagine seeing every person not only as a human being but with love. What effort. Imagination is the first way out of tragic patterns, where the threads squeeze our necks.

o o o

Loving the woman with the weeping baby.
Loving the man with one leg and barely a voice to speak.
Loving the voices whose words we don't understand.
Relentless, shocking wonder of love.

o o o

The threads might change if, alliterative, the lyric-founding founders discovered love, the examples of the inalienable rights in founding a nation. The pursuit of happiness suggests many things and the liberty to pursue that which leads to the ambiguous "happiness."

What rights are worth protecting, and what does declaring them mean to our values?

o o o

The Europeans who arrived read the Bible often and repeated it, in sermons and in lessons, making reading a value for all colonial New England boys and girls. The gift of reading was given to all, while instruction in writing was extended to boys only. Who creates our stories and shapes the telling is not a puzzle. In Ecclesiastes we would read that all is vanity, and that which is has already been.

o o o

The face I loved and never touched is still one connection of gentle possibility that pushes against the possibility of terror. The possibility of loving, even loving dissembled, builds networks that see. I saw you then, through a crowd, at a distance, and I loved you. I saw you nearby, at my side, in a conversation. Now, I might see you everywhere. Mirrors multiplying the fragmented image, like broken shards.

o o o

Given the grandness of the claims to eternity, the burden of temporality of love on earth can feel heavy. The easing of this burden may be the man trying to escape from loving. This is that mistake, Kierkegaard's deception. To love may be heavy, but it is strange to imagine that to avoid the burden would be a relief. The value of ease for myself cannot be sustained. My self is not isolated. "The detached observer is as much entangled as the active participant."

o o o

Lovelessness is a boon to consumerism. — bell hooks

I do not need to hold your face to love. I remember you, standing at a distance under a bright light in some concentration. I remember you, sitting close as spring emerged among the trees. Memory entangled with the book entangled with tomorrow and some impossible knowing.

I don't need to buy it or sell it. I don't need to hold it captive.

o o o

If I don't stop to ponder the love, does it need exercise? Might it go weak or slack like an unused muscle?

Meanwhile, epidemic urgency for productivity steals devotion to thinking, to thinking about love. For love will only be thought well in dwelling. If we find no place to dwell in, we are lost, too.

"No city to dwell in" is what Bradford found, landing the Mayflower. He wanted to make a place to dwell in a place he found but not loving.

You wrestle with love, its alienation from you, its inconsistency, until
the notion of its familiarity is blurred, disconnected from the intimacy
of love with our very being, our experience, ourselves, wherein love
is and acts and bodies forth. There must be a simplicity to love that
stuns, too.

Shimmering thread.

Blurring, confusion, disappointment. It sounds like the language of
desire. Desire is what is longed for, reached for, not quite grasped.
Love might be different.

o o o

I can live with the person I love, sometimes forgetting the urgency
of new love, the way the body shifts between panic and ease, alarm
and promise. Loving, these are all latent, the mountain resting still
above the volcano. Vesuvius appears far away from the still summer
air at Pompeii. I am loving alert to that seismic activity, even the most
subtle movements seep out a reminder.

In love, the ease can feel like calm, almost like nothing, but its quiet
pleasures can be intensified by what could bubble up. Potential.

"You're going for a walk? Now?" He leans forward in the chair, folding

over knees to reach the laces. *"Is something wrong?"* A hint at alarm. Nothing's wrong. "I've been inside too long." And "It's a beautiful day out, finally." "I need a little exercise." And "You inspire me." The love is mixed in with all its potential disruptions. They make it what it becomes, in contrast but also in concert.

○ ○ ○

How can I write a poem for someone else's wedding if my love is so original, so private, so wholly ours? It cannot be mine. To love must be entangled. To love otherwise is not loving, but may be slipping close to love's threads, netted. Then again, it may be different. "Powerless to utter itself, powerless to speak, love nonetheless wants to proclaim itself, to exclaim, to write itself everywhere."

○ ○ ○

> Mist fills the air and turns the sky
> A warm gray we walk
> At the same time on different
> Streets noticing the dimming
> Light, feeling a moistening air slow
> Breathing the wet in I want
> To tell you looks like rain
> But you already know
> I tell you anyway knowing
> you know, like I love you.

o o o

"Despair is to lack the eternal," Kierkegaard tells us. He continues, "despair consists in not having undergone the transformation of the eternal through duty's 'You shall.' Despair is not, therefore the loss of the beloved — that is misfortune, pain, and suffering; but despair is the lack of the eternal".

This sense of duty in relation to love, to loving — *you shall love* — distinguishes the love that connects us to "the eternal" rather than fleeting, temporal love, the "spontaneous," love that dances with despair. His language of "the eternal" evokes a relationship to time and space that can meet and blur with thinking that makes room for secular and skeptical thought even within his devotion to Christian study. This important eternal is capacious and flexible understanding crucial to experience, what is not temporal, linear, or limited but interrelated, imprecisely imagined yet nonetheless understood and necessarily abstract.

o o o

Do you remember the time when we ate that meal or went together to see this band in concert, or we had that conversation? No, I don't remember. But I know the slope of the field behind the stadium. I know how the light fell just so after dusk. And the feel of the water in the glass, not quite cold, not quite warm.

What faces I hold, to love beyond their place in my days. The beloved faces I do not touch mix my past with a future drawn clear only by thought, feeling, and loving attention: dwelling.

o o o

It is hard to detach the unloving dictates of some scriptural passages with the loving words of others. In the Bible, clear words appear on how men and women should wear their hair so as not to be degrading, just before the words "[love] does not insist on its own way."

o o o

That love, as duty, is connected to "the eternal" is an important emphasis in the *Works of Love*, changing love from feeling or emotion, to something central to a lived experience that makes understood one's part in the network of loving and time. Living and the afterlife, linked. The relational nature of love is both connected to the individual and beloved and simultaneously something larger, the eternal, and this is both a feeling, love, and a duty, you shall love, and these are not separate, but entangled and necessarily so to "be secured against despair."

There is, to be sure, plenty of despair.

What security do we seek "against despair" but love must do more? It entangles or reveals the entanglements.

o o o

Sitting cross-legged on my purple carpet, as a young girl I stared and stared at that photo of Brian under the pine trees in a Massachusetts state park. What once was wilderness, now dotted with picnic tables. I tried to see some signal, but the blurry photo was inert. My attention looking through that camera lens had gone unnoticed on that cloudy field trip, or worse unwelcome, embarrassing. Kids' loving goes unnoticed, embarrassing, and later becomes an embarrassment of riches. Tender memory, unexpected grief. The long threads of love reach in unruly directions.

o o o

Different stories would create different mythologies. Can we imagine a founding myth of generosity? Love means something to us, but I have seen its power shunned as if to claim "love!" is weakness. I care more about you than is mythologized. Life, liberty, and the pursuit of love, I say.

o o o

Loving the friend who opens my letter,
And loving the friend who never writes back.
Loving the boy on the field trip.
Loving his parents, who keep secrets, loving.

Love and liberty get knotted as we write the words. "To speak starting from the already known also paralyzes the becoming of the one and of the other," warns Irigaray in "The Sharing of Speech" in *The Way of Love*. Can love become the possibility of something new, a provocation to imagine? Sharing, speaking, loving.

There will be no wild celebration for loving embrace.

And there will be the loving embrace.

○ ○ ○

The tender touch of the mother prepares us. The caring call from a friend prepares us. All of it, preparation for love, its potential.

○ ○ ○

Sign my letter, *With Love, Leah*. For years I couldn't do it. Each time I wrote, I would stop and ask, *Am I feeling love right now? Is this loving? Is my letter sent with love?* It pained me to sign a false note, or to write a cold ending. What does this mean *With Love?* To merely be polite? Whose manners depend on a diluting of feeling and a spreading of gentle lies? Maybe, young, I was loving a little too intensely, not with enough duty.

○ ○ ○

More liberty, more memory. Love won't be just a thing to find at all.

○ ○ ○

The slow attention insists on care. To attempt some attention is an affection — a recognition of connection. We might call it a duty. Some cubist portrait I create to see what the pieces make in their broken, entangling beauty.

> *Where does this tenderness come from?*
> *And what shall I do with it, young*
> *sly singer, just passing by?*
> *Your lashes are — longer than anyone's.*
>   Marina Tsvetaeva

Thread: *Riddle of Peace*

> If learning were a path of wisdom,
> those most learned about myth
> would not believe, with Hesiod,
> that Pallas in her wisdom gloats
> over the noise of battle.
>
> Heraclitus, trans. B. Haxton

Peace is as water: everywhere not to be made but to find, harness, recognize. To make peace is to live peacefully. The very work is a slippery liquid, water cupped in the palm that glides through the fingers as we raise it to drink. Wet palm, we see it but remain thirsty.

The troubled ways of writing peace: it is already, not to be created. Violence is what we make. Peace is often written as negation: non-violence or anti-war. The bruised language, the already broken path. Logic makes violence the given or standard against which we make peace.

Entangled with its very undoing.

o o o

The American emphasis on the language of freedom in early colonial history is a story entangled with slavery. Freedom means not being enslaved, yet champions of freedom owned slaves. Freedom means freedom from bondage, of the mind, of the body, of the imagination. Champions of freedom kept human beings from freedom by contract, by law, by force, and by design. How? Why? The answers emerge: excuses, ugly. How can we reach for peace with wrists shackled or shackling?

○ ○ ○

Understanding peace is to understand the possibility of radical peace. This is where thought led Einstein: brighter, hotter. The threads entangle, impossible to unravel, or only so far. Too far, for now.

Close up, things look different than they might from a distance.

○ ○ ○

I lived with a man who often greeted strangers on the street. He was called friendly, and this was a generous gesture of connection with the world. It was also a kind of protection.

I have walked the same streets in quiet contemplation without greeting the same strangers. I am at peace with our relation and non-violence, and I give generous span to my neighbors' privacy. Or I say hello.

There are many ways to make peace. There are many ways to love.

○ ○ ○

"And, as the prestige of language falls, that of silence rises," wrote
Susan Sontag. Sometimes we will not know how to speak, or what to
say, or why.

○ ○ ○

"Though enslaved people never made up more than 5 or 10% of the
population in New England's largest town, and far less than in rural
areas, they nonetheless played a significant role in keeping the region's
premodern economy functioning and growing."

One is not insignificant.

○ ○ ○

Wounds get clotted. Except sometimes they don't. The blood will not
stop, and the spilling, even the leaking is dangerous. Some people are
known to die of the bleeding. Some people are at risk of unstoppable
bleeding every time a wound pierces enough to bleed.

Be gentle with each other. Strength is not always adequate. Formulas
for survival are not formulas at all. Are not the same survivals.

○ ○ ○

It is not far reading in the Bible to find justifications of slavery. Slaves abound, as Cotton Mather, the cruel and powerful New England minister knew. The description of the faithful slave or the unfaithful slave in Matthew. In Ephesians — "Slave, obey ... " "Whether we are slaves or free ... "

According to the Bible, we divorced and remained adulterers. A strange kind of forgiveness to decipher.

 "Love your enemies." — Luke 6:35

o o o

Stand or rest and what stands with you? Peace.

Imagine being soaked in peace.

o o o

The stories we tell shape the world we inhabit. The stories we tell have largely been arguments for violence. In the founding decades of the New England colonies, colonists recorded encounters with the occult, and these shaped the world. Horses were bewitched. People could be harmed at a distance by witchcraft. When a figure appeared unrecognizable, visions and apparitions were linked to "black magic." An enslaved man in 1679 Salem reported being suspicious of black cats.

o o o

I tell the story of a person who wanted a child and was offered a child's hand to hold, and that hand was open to love. True, they were tired from wounds and medications and myths. "How can I love what is not mine?" the childless one asked, and then she refused the hand.

Who is ever "mine"? What person? In love the hand must ever be opening, opening. I love you. I am trying to love you. All.

Mythologies of the enemy hurting the righteous make it possible to imagine violence. So many stories.

What makes it possible to imagine retreat? Imagine the open hand.

I too wanted a child to love, to live with. I too blinked in the work of making-it-happen. Love is work of a different order. Being a parent and loving are not synonymous here — how could they be with all the brutal evidence to the contrary? Violence depends on depersonalization. Do you see your child?

I too wanted a child and took the pills and measured the body and injected the hormones to make it happen. But it happens, the wanting and the having, the terror at losing something that doesn't yet exist becoming the terror of losing what you hold in your arms and then help learn to walk and then watch walk away. Every change is impossible then it is possible then it is. Okay, so I cry then I laugh, or almost. I'm sad and empty then I'm pregnant and afraid, alienated by my own body. Then I'm alone again, or never alone again for the rest of my life, because once you become a mother you are always a mother, even if you lose your child or your mind or your life. And I still don't know where the threshold is. Khaled Hosseini composed this beautiful sentence, and it sings in me: "I wondered if that was how forgiveness budded; not with the fanfare of epiphany, but with pain gathering its things, packing up, and slipping away unannounced in the middle of the night." When does the most profound feeling cross a threshold? The bud emerging from the earth or this water seeping into the ground. Impossible to measure.

Violence is an intimacy too. You are there, touched, struck.

How are we to know what doesn't touch us? What doesn't hurt may not seem to touch us. How can we prevent a violence we don't see and can't feel? It must need imagination. Pain gathering its things.

○ ○ ○

The poetry imagines and investigates the murder of Africans on a slave ship. In *Zong!* #12 we read:

                it

                        is said
                        has been decided
                        was justified

appeared impossible
is not necessary
is another ground
need not be proved

And we understand that the poet, M. NourbeSe Philip, is teaching us to pay attention to patterns. The poet is writing of the enslaved people, the murdered people on the slave ship.

"was justified"

o o o

Books are written by men who repeat over and over that war, brutality, cruelty of violence is inevitable, is so old and familiar and repeated that it must be a requisite part of life. And yet, imagine if we confront this story. All the stories.

"I would like to write a book about war that would make war sickening, and the very thought of it repulsive. Insane ... So that even the generals would be sickened. // My men friends (as opposed to women) are taken aback by such 'women's' logic. And again I hear the 'men's' argument: 'You weren't in the war.' But maybe that's a good thing: I don't know the passion of hatred; my vision is normal. Unwarlike, unmanly." And Svetlana Alexievich goes on to share such stories. Before the book even begins, mothers are drowning their own babies, men are raping young girls. So many died, covered in blood. So many shared the stories of murder.

She collects the stories of women who fought in the Second World War. She wins a Nobel Prize for her efforts, decades later. "Courage in war and courage in thought are two different courages. I used to think they were the same."

o o o

I go to the market to buy milk, I will not hurt you, grocer. And if the ways our words and movements intersect and make space for it, the connection will be kind, will be another entanglement. To be violent makes action that disturbs connection. Anti-peace.

Passersby push. I am bumped by your shoulder. Where you struck me, passerby, it hurts, but this is not violence.

An opportunity for loving entanglement.

What will you choose?

o o o

"We reach out our hand to our rifle in the darkness of the trenches and we recognize it as an archaic gesture, infinitely older than History, a savage, primordial gesture whose essence hasn't been altered by the shells, the gas attacks, the planes, and all the monstrous efforts of modernity, because nothing will ever alter it." In Ferrari's novel *The Principle*, we enter the life of the physicist who breaks the world even as he seeks to know it. Whose infinity is he telling?

We are the scientist. We are the philosopher. We are the creators of the atomic bomb. We are the soldier and the Nazi and the dissident. But I am not included in this vision. Whose story am I being entangled in, choked by the threads?

○ ○ ○

What was not now is: the baby appears who had not been before. A skin smooth nearly liquid in its softness. The baby is mine and not mine. I pull the softest tiny shirt over the softest skin.

The before and after of the tiny body resting on my large body can be offered as a time on a clock, on a calendar, but the time before the tiny fingernails cuts lines into my face is changed by the appearance of the baby, the eyes, the body, the tightly holding fingers. The appearance of the baby becomes a new kind of measure.

○ ○ ○

In the bibliography of the Stanford Encyclopedia of Philosophy entry on Pacifism, revised in 2014, there are more than 80 authors named. Of these, I can identify five women's names. The percentage of works cited is even lower, since some of the men have two, three, four, as many as seven books listed.

○ ○ ○

You decide to notice: It emerges that the woman is struggling to write, wants to tell her husband she is tired, she is afraid; imagine this struggle becomes a battle. And in your own streets, or with the in-laws, with the children, you begin to see the persistent battles. Battling to remember, to see, or mostly to forget, to let it slide. The woman writing reminds us of the Republic, who had rights and who didn't in the ancient Greek democracies we celebrate. The women were left behind. The slaves had no rights. Who are you in this history? What role are you playing, reader? Are we still astonished when she takes the time to read Plato, to respond to Kant, to question your Nietzsche? What battles are really worth fighting?

In this letter, a lifetime of wakeful duty confronted.

Does paying attention to the past differently change the present?

○ ○ ○

Every moment becomes a before, and every moment becomes after or now or when. The birth, the death, the blossoming and fading — wondrous, thrilling, sad, confusing. The urgency of wanting peace extends beyond my immediate surroundings, stretches to everywhere this new person might go, every bit of air she might breathe. What was imaginary becomes a person and vulnerability becomes less abstract. When the baby's fingers touch my face, I'm a little bit afraid.

○ ○ ○

Zong! #12 continues:

> it
>
> was a throwing overboard
>
> it
>
> is a particular circumstance
>
> need not be proved
>
> is another ground
>
> is not necessary
>
> appeared impossible
>
> was justified
>
> has been decided
>
> is said
>
> it
>
> was

○ ○ ○

The fear mingling with love extends beyond my body, touching the tender baby body. It must, or I will forget to love you. To protect you, reader, is to protect the baby.

○ ○ ○

If no one will read the work, then does it exist? Many trees falling, becoming silent paper, books.

o   o   o

Water slips through your fingers.

o   o   o

We call a certain kind of loss "throwing out the baby with the bath water." No one would ever do that.

o   o   o

A glance at the Pacifism bibliography reveals the binary nature of the study. Most books about peace are books about war. Ethics, religion, and non-violence come up, too. But mostly war. And never love. Not in this list.

o   o   o

In the bookstore, there are many books — rows and rows of them — on war. These books are categorized by conflict, by region, by date. There are books on theories of war and histories of war. I ask the clerk to help me find "peace studies." Help me find books on "pacifism." I ask this here and there, now and then, in any bookstore. There is never a section. I am directed to the social history section or philosophy or cultural studies. I am directed to all the books on war. In January, there are MLK books on display. But every day, row after row: The Civil War, the World Wars, The Perfect Weapon, The Perfect Soldier, The Perfect Battle, Guantanamo ... My utopian shelf has the browser encountering peaceful images alongside these.

I want to know about the violence, to heal, and to know about the peace, to imagine.

○ ○ ○

Preparing the reader for the oral history the Soviet women tell of war, Alexievich explains:

"We didn't know a world without war; the world of war was the only one familiar to us, and the people of war were the only people we knew. Even now I don't know any other world and any other people. Did they ever exist?"

○ ○ ○

And you have a baby. You want a baby. Or you don't want a baby. Or you were a baby. Or the baby never came. The lack of the baby is another tenderness. The loss of the baby another vulnerability. Times before and times after. You don't want to hear about the baby. Who cares about your baby? It crushes the abstraction of the imagination.

But look, her eyes are wet, look a tooth is poking through the pink gums, listening, she's opening tiny lips to speak.

o o o

The Africans on the Zong were murdered at sea. Thrown overboard.
The court case described in the poem was over an insurance claim.

appeared impossible
.was justified

o o o

Stories shape our experiences, as we encounter the stories, and we
encounter each other.

We can't disentangle ourselves from the violence.
What we say about violence.
What we do not say.

o o o

Imagine being soaked in peace.

o o o

If the book begets the book, ideas sprout new ideas from their projections, then the lack of peace books, the bounty in books on war — even those asking why, those claiming injustice and outrage! — must be entangled in the books to come. The ideas of outrage, how will they bring ideas of peace?

o o o

The open hand.

The quiet passerby.

The freely crying baby.

Pages of books flying, flying, filling the sky.

Pages of books flying, catching the light.

In every language, swinging feathers of wonder, words and more words

Falling pages wildly flying, landing, finding the open hand, at the end of the arm,

Attached to the body, feeling the altered air.

Thread: *The Book*

> [We] can say that the very act of reading opens the possibility
> of an ethical space or encounter, one that signals our
> willingness to be changed or transformed by what we read.
>
> Michelle Boulous Walker

If the book isn't written, it cannot be read.

In response to the world, I write. In response to how the world
intersects with the body, I write. In response to loss, I write. In
response to wonder, I write. Black notebooks, unlined pages, black
felt-tip pen. I write.

There are pieces, bubbles that form, float visibly, then float away or
burst or both. There is no line, no narrative memory but connecting
these floating pieces might form a shape. Rarely, a bubble does settle
on a surface, easily examined but this is momentary too. By now,
I know the pace, the temporality of memory. Even those that feel
so startlingly fixed, so settled, too will break. Maybe a residue of
the bubble will remain, slick and a bit dangerous, then more slowly
evaporating.

To write means writing, putting words on the page.

Ink dries. Sharp pencil grows soft.

○ ○ ○

Even when I'm exhausted, the threads come together. It is not always clear whence they come or if moving. They, I, the thought. What my abstraction here is meant to communicate is an understanding of how a thought — any given thought — is a mingling of many parts, and even this, its recognition, is not fixed or static, its parts not known. We all might or do recognize this.

Bergson starts *Creative Evolution* with an observation, simple enough, about the constancy of change. From the plainness of this — the plainness of its complexities — emerges a flattening, relentlessly. What was the lively bubble, its wetness dries on the page into a stain. Words on the page.

What is wild and messy is made tidy, or at least appears so. The knotting quipus. The neat lines printed and stitched into a book.

I'm trying to say that the page contains a change and is changed by its contents.

I'm trying to say that women read books by men.

We are changed by what we read. Do we concentrate on Jane's telling us "I longed for a power of vision which might overpass that limit" or the final page's "Reader, I married him"? Did I read this before or after my first heartbreak? Wasn't the true romance of the book swirling in

Jane Eyre's longing to reach beyond the confines of her small world?

o o o

If god calls upon the people we call puritans to be free and that
freedom expands sprawling like a gas, like a fragrance, then that would
be quite liberating, free-making. People lived and tried to explain a
number of things in Massachusetts in the 17th century by a system
of thinking described as radically contingent thought. For the same
puritans the Bible justified the buying of people, the enslavement of
human beings, the very not-free-making of people.

Contingencies often attempt to tidy up what is messy. The mess is far
more humane, but harder to navigate. Again and again, the echo: "His
culture amounts to a sort of monologue more and more extrapolated
from the real, unfolding itself parallel to this real in order to carve it up
and thus dominate it."

o o o

What we call a book began with thought, imagination, idea, and
became the object in my hand. The book is heavy but not too heavy to
pass around, carry with us. I put a book in my tote bag before I leave
my apartment, lock the door behind me. I might read it. The book is
this potential.

o o o

Divine love is something we can only speculate about, yet that speculation makes human love legible. Or it is the experience of love in human interaction that enables us to imagine — to speculate about — the possibility of a divine love. Love has the qualities of power, and love and power exist outside the realm of logic or even apprehension at all.

Yet it is written. Something fixed on a page.

○ ○ ○

The reading will not tell you how to think, for you think already.

Alter a path or form an intersection with a thought you kept elsewhere. Do you even know what you know? Do you notice how you are noticing? The book creates the book, and the thought creates the thought, so too opening to the page creates an opening, where you decide, I am open to this change.

We walk hand-in-hand into the large stone building. The museum tells us that people first kept logs of things, catalogs, registers. But we see stories, we see poems, we do what is called making-sense. The words are not ours. Some of the words are pictures — hieroglyphs or paintings or shapes carved into stones or the stones themselves arranged into shapes. There are many things, ways we might understand as language. The words change, but there is little evidence to show they improve. We turn back pages and find many marks, fading, in the palimpsest. We can read or we can only see a curled line, a wavy line that becomes water around the clay pot. We can feel the effort to say or record or speak. What tells us better about how to look than the stone arranged in a circle, catching the shadow of the sun?

The museum tells us the wavy lines mean water. I call the child over: *Look at this pattern: wavy lines. They tell us this pot was used for water.* The child looks, patiently, impatiently. The child looks away, curious about other things. *What are these?* pointing to early sculptures of comic erotic scenes.

If the book isn't written, it cannot be read.

The changes may be ours, and private writing in the dark of morning. We insist on a narrative so we might wrest control, when we are but living. Attempting to notice part of what is available to notice, to take in, to grasp. It is not the work of people to control it all — it all, at all. This is the great misunderstanding. To speak is not to harness. To name is not to own.

○ ○ ○

Having touched my body to other bodies, the sculptures startle me with their exaggerated body parts, large and unsubtle and ugly. I laugh. Such very large protuberances! The child's confusion provokes curiosity, my smile, a squeeze of tenderness.

Not afraid of wonder: Am I harder to control when I spread in thought, uncontained and ill suited to containment? Yet wonder keeps me gentle. There is beauty in the tenderness of wonder. Were wildness to become a gentle perceiving of wonder, rather than a pushing or kicking back against some constraints, would wildness need taming? Wild, wild wonder.

○ ○ ○

I ask students to record what they encounter in a notebook. Write details, idle observations. After a few months, students say *I never realized how much I am noticing*. Or they say *I never realized how much I am not paying attention to*.

Not to be dismayed or astonished but to know we might go back, pass over the page in the book again, see and read the words again. We missed something. We always did. And it has changed since then. And will again, to our astonishment, if we are lucky.

○ ○ ○

Open to wonder in hopes of being loveable and loving, does this soften the hand that would strike? Violence depends on depersonalization. This curtailing love's wonder is another way of putting space between ourselves and others. Of adding distance. What of the child struck by his own mother? How far away is he under that touch?

○ ○ ○

Separating words, the living room becomes something else. The living, the room, with space between the words to understand something about how this space, this room, is not just a living room, but a room for living, of living, a not-dying room, an alive room. No longer the room where we lay our dead. I want to be in it, the living room, I want to crack wide that space between the words and make its aliveness more vivid. And all words connecting might expand like this, an explosion that could burst with possibility, poetry, but is yet there each and every time we say I-am-going-to-the-living-room. Is the book in the living room? Let's clean the living room. Let's enter it.

○ ○ ○

"But what if language expresses as much by what is between words as by the words themselves? By what it does not 'say' as by what it 'says'?"

Maurice Merleau-Ponty   ✿

○ ○ ○

The sleepy, the tired mind is challenged to grasp the words in the book. The very same words on the very same page do not fix themselves in thought. Where do they go, or do they not go, as the eye passes over the words, almost hearing sounds of words but not shaping the thoughts, or not quite holding them together? To read without reading, to see without seeing, to think without thinking. Much of living passes in this way. The tired mind has difficulty grasping the words in thought, returns over them again, again. But this return is only the exercise of effort, the push of attention, whereas lacking these, the words barely exist, the encounter is the non-encounter, something else is happening or has passed.

Will I turn the page? Will I return to the passage? Will I pass over? Has it been read?

What in life outside of reading is so elusive and so shimmering? Can we be astonished by most of it? We are reading the world as we live it — or we must. How astonishing to consider all we miss, when, paying attention, everything multiplies, multiplies again. Large, explaining, and minute, down to microscopic vision or invisible, memory and those, the other memories and interference. That waking-up that illuminates all the rest, rest that we sleep through.

○ ○ ○

To look is to seek but also to recognize what more must be and the impossibility of knowing, or its excess, beyond reach of eye and mind.

Vision is held as the window to knowledge (elsewhere), as metaphor or not even as metaphor. It is suspicious. Vision and knowledge, both. We might be wise to puzzle more over what we know, and what we see.

Jabès puts vision in the language of destruction. God in blindness. The invisibility and a knowledge beyond sight. Maybe this is wisdom. It is beyond, too, words. Yet in the book.

o o o

A monologue is talking without interaction, without entanglement. Another philosopher writes, "His culture amounts to a sort of monologue," and then she observes more. This monologue is a form of domination. She continues, "His culture amounts to a sort of monologue more and more extrapolated from the real, unfolding itself parallel to this real in order to carve it up and thus dominate it." The more detached, or disentangled, the word pretends to be, the more its effort to oppress. The effort is sometimes called an achievement. "This is not very respectful of the other. And it does not lead to happiness. Neither does it correspond to a human wisdom, but rather to an exile surrounded by fortifications where man takes shelter. One of the instruments of use to him for constructing this enclosure is language itself." Language of monologue, of exile, of exclusion, of exclosure.

Recognize another kind of prison. To dominate, the world is "carved up" into parts, the parts named and separated, but the separating also separates the one putting up those fortifications. You, who would tell me the right way to write how I know, what I feel, where and when my experiences put heavy weight on that knowledge, where and what wisdom emerges: You put up the fortress to keep my wisdom out, too.

Call it "lawlessness." Call it "banished." Witchcraft.

Or typing your monologue does not connect us. Where is your wonder?

o o o

I don't know what I said about the large phallic sculptures in the museum. Ridiculous is what I thought. Maybe *looks painful*. I suspect this is not what was first thought by the sculptor. Then again, there's a lot I don't know. Then again, still ridiculous.

o o o

When I wrote my own story in adolescence, I was not Careful Jane but a mermaid — wild, violent, mysterious. I wrote a story of a temptation that sucks you, sailor, into the ocean.

o o o

Resisting the allure of mastery is some kind of wisdom. "Naming what we are also is imperative without aspiring to master the whole, without thus mastering ourselves through and through." The push to mastery, to be master of, even in the book, to make the understanding appear whole and mastered, is a false promise and the crown sought by an oppressor.

What are alternative ways of speaking, naming that does not seek to master, does not claim to master a whole or ignore the gaps that shape experience? What invites and interacts with the reaches, the spaces, of energy, possibility, of what does not yet connect or have language but might? A poetics of entanglement.

Irigaray names it "difference itself" as necessarily "giving up its artificial and authoritarian unity." Unity dissipates and becomes difference. But this kind of difference is there already, dancing, in every connection.

Your seeing of this glass of water on this table is not my seeing of this glass or this very table, and even what you say of it as I hear it changes what I see. Am I able to listen? Our poems, our words might conjure yet other water, other thirst.

The book is naming in another way — of what is and isn't and the spaces that are and shift — without fixing such a specificity that assumes a totality, that appropriates the space, the room for others.

"The object may remain the same, I may look at it from the same side, at the same angle, in the same light; nevertheless, the vision I now have of it differs from that which I have just had, even if only because the one is an instant older than the other." Bergson begins.

What claim could we have for mastery, and further for mastery of what is outside that shifting light?

○ ○ ○

"Lawlessness seen as negligence is at first feminized and then restricted or banished." We might call the lawlessness freedom. We might call negligence experiment. This is observed in Susan Howe's *The Birth-mark* on page one of a study of American literature. Justifications of our banishment are rooted in language and the body at once. Feminize freedoms taken as wrong. To be woman is to become vulnerable. Feminize is to minimize.

○ ○ ○

The light in the museum is diffused. Today the translucent shades are drawn down the large windows, protecting pages of old books from the light. Ancient papers rest under glass. My neck feels a tightening under my right shoulder. Why did I bring so many books on this outing?

○ ○ ○

Living room was once the parlor, and this room is where the dead were laid. The room of the dead was moved out, formally, to the funeral parlor. And the room of the dead becomes the living room.

I tidy up. I put out a vase of wild blue flowers I can't name. I've never been good with flora and fauna. Sit down to write.

o o o

Some years ago, I wrote a poem and called it "A conception is a motion." Later, I entangled this poem with John Cage, who said, "There is no such thing as silence." Later still, I read the poem for friends on their wedding day. A conception is a motion. The book begets the book.

As you speak, I will listen; as you write, I will read. This is an understanding of transcendence, because we can approach the ways of seeing the glass on the table, or the water within it, or yet the shadow it casts to the side in this light. But it is only a nearing.

"Everything is again set in motion — called into question — by writing. As we speak, nothing is ever said so completely that it could not be said over, differently. So that saying is a revelation, with the promise of further saying," promises Jabès in the *Book of Margins*. One wonders if there is any more important part of a page.

Words transcend the distance, or but approach that transcending. To believe in the work is to approach, too, is to listen more than to speak. The poem, even as we write it, is also a listening.

We imagine walking across a desert. We imagine a mirage. I have never been to the desert, not with these legs, these eyes, this skin. The mirage is always a work of the mind, and even this I am imagining.

"Only in fragments can we read the immeasurable totality. Hence it is with reference to a fabricated totality that we tackle a fragment, which always represents the accepted, traditional part of the totality, yet at the same time renews its challenge of the beginning and, taking its place, becomes the beginning of all possible beginnings that can be brought to light." Jabès again.

○ ○ ○

A conception is a motion.

To begin. There is always the light. (Before the light there were many things, but in darkness.) The way it swells from the lamp. The way it squints from the blinds, shut tightly. To begin with the light sends a chill along my arms. Begin with the arms. Exposed, pale, weak. Begin with the arms in motion — reaching. Begin with the reaching toward. It is the reaching toward that swells the tears and this the urge again to begin. Since the early years, it has been a reaching toward. Even my [   ] is a mystery I am always reaching toward. And the unborn — ~~the~~ — that could fill those slowly lifting arms, those arms like orange ribbons blowing behind a tall kite. Begin with the motion, then, but where? The moving eye, the lifted hand, the breaking glass, the running pigeon, the blowing newsprint. Begin with the moving eye. That is, the light.

○ ○ ○

The newspaper of record piles up a list of men accused of something the child wants defined. *What does this mean, Mama, predator?* You know, it's an animal that goes after prey, like when we see a falcon flying above the forest, it's looking for food, then it swoops down. Maybe it catches a rabbit or a smaller animal, its prey. The falcon is the predator. *Oh Mama.* Why do you ask? *I read it here in the magazine — sexual-predator.*

It's a slightly modified explanation then, but more or less the same. Replace smaller-animal with other-person's-body.

o o o

Does each assertion of a poetics of justice have to assert itself loudly? Just listen. It's in many things, in a steady voice.

In a steady voice. Is urgency ignored heard in a steady voice?

Leave space to consider the claims. The assertions.

o o o

The story we tell about man's natural violence is itself man's violence and is a story we tell.

I read other stories.

The stories change. And now I remember so vividly the part often passed over, forgotten, ignored. Jane said no to St. John. "I am ready to go to India if I may go free." And so, she doesn't go at all.

○ ○ ○

To learn how to read is to become careful with what reading can do. Careful might mean loving. Careful might mean slow. Tender. Careful might mean deliberate or purposeful. With care toward something other than reading itself. This is learning how to read. Reading goes beyond reading. This explains its relationship to entanglement. The ironic evidence of the linear sentences, word after word on the page. The intriguing spaces between them all, marking so many choices, other words not written.

If the only book you ever read is the Bible, then you will believe the Bible is the only book that can change you profoundly.

○ ○ ○

The reader tells me the poems are sad.
A listener tells me the poems are stunning. Enough to make her cry.
Another says the poem breaks your heart, they are so, you know,
    so moving.
That's enough.
Give a detail it makes it easier.
Easier how.

Easier to understand.
I stop. If the reader is weeping, what more is there to understand?

o o o

I must have read this long ago: "Including every secret thing."
Ecclesiastes. In youth, in years when secrets were magic, were quiet,
were dangerous, wholly mine. Every word of this book is familiar.
Where did it go?

o o o

The complicated violence against Dinah in the Bible, the violence
that violence provokes, and the many acts since. Built up and broken
down, Dinah. What are we learning? Stories writers have been telling
and we have been reading and hearing for so long. Since this version
of beginning.

To write of love must mean a return to both the book and the body.

o o o

Damp air. White sky we call gray, overcast. The clouds lifting. Day
brightening. Summer's end.

Turn out toward the rest and the ear awakens to sound. A chirping
becomes a wheeling moan, and endless urgent crickets make

silence impossible. Is silence even possible? Once we hear it, we are muttering over it in our minds at least.

Maybe in the explosions of love.

Grateful to have lived so long and be living in such bodily silences. I read the words of my own intensity, some true moment, truly of the body and out of it, and that truth read, intensity coming through the page, in words, as familiar in spite of its unfamiliarity. Who is this Leah who felt this sweat, who looked at this dangling apple? Now, years later and experiences past, no less true. More truly familiar. Reading becomes an affirmation of a knowing before knowing.

Books work on this epistemology, mostly. How do we know knowing? Words are given to us to understand, to grasp at some knowing that is not our own yet comes from someone's being and our sensitivity to it. The writer can bring us closer to their knowing, or their near-knowing, their grasping-knowing, grappling-knowing, longing-knowing. Then we enter into some question, some new familiar.

Even my own poem is not my own, entangled with memory, life, a poetic uncertainty principle.

○ ○ ○

Squealing insects' intensity like a siren. Then the blur of an overhead plane. Distant traffic. A power tool sharpens, ripping into wood with lowering growls. Finally, voices, bubbling, young, far. The city, its comforting wildness ordered, feels less distant by increments. Its mill builds up to calm routine. The chaos of the disconnected mind bit by bit, traced and encircled until it becomes a form. A form: something we recognize and can share.

Sound's distance makes (some) sense — both within us, heard, and happening outside us, made. We can hear but the sound is apart from us, made by the world. Yet the sound — noise, music, loudness or whispering hushes, almost-not-heard little shifts — exists for us only insomuch as we hear it. So too all the world.

The raucous quiet of under trees in summer — birds, even their wings a rush of sound, and rattling songs, the constant scratching of insects, the breeze noisily agitating branches — will feel always like a return, if you ever have sat there, listened, noticed. Attending to this other world returns you to what? Another moment of reflection? A broken heart? A decision to be brave? A grateful recognition? An almost recognizable confusion? Are you with me? And it slips away, too, the moment, as this new one becomes the moment — the listening drifting into elsewhere, the slowing familiar of attention to world, to other, to relations, to self, to entanglement.

Thread: *Riddle of the Physical*

> We choose to examine a phenomenon which is impossible,
> *absolutely* impossible, to explain in any classical way, and which
> has in it the heart of quantum mechanics. In reality, it contains
> the only mystery. We cannot explain the mystery in the sense
> of 'explaining' how it works. We will *tell* you how it works.
>
> Richard Feynman, "Quantum Behavior"

A poetics implicit in discovery is embodied in the pause, attention
to the atom or the eye or memory, the carefully recorded finding of
the laboratory.

The scientific article reminds us that questions reveal new areas
yet unknown, we are relentlessly discovering that we know little,
what we knew was mistaken, knowledge is nothing compared to the
unknown, and what we call known is unstable, uncertain, is more like
potential than precision. Science is filled with language of "potential"
and "uncertainty."

Everything reminds me that questions reveal new areas yet unknown.
I am relentlessly discovering that I know little, that what I knew was
mistaken. "I wish I hadn't tried to seem like I knew everything back
when we were younger," says Abby over Zoom on a cold January
morning. "I would have learned so much more if I'd admitted I don't
know things."

The reflecting scientist insists again and again on entangling it in our everyday understanding of science and the world itself — what scientists study.

How the brain functions.
How the atoms interact.
How bodies move.
What we imagine and what we see.

A poetics of illogic knowing is increasingly recognized. "The task is to see the riddle," Heidegger wrote, thinking about art, perception, being in the world.

○ ○ ○

Each noun in Einstein's writing is held up as a question, is loosened from its place of master knowledge, and this we recognize as, finally, genius. The name Einstein redefining this word, revealing its very instability. Reading the last sentence in chapter four of The Special Theory of Relativity, the eyes blur, not in confusion, but in the wet of recognition. "The laws of mechanics of Galilei-Newton can be regarded as valid only for a Galileian system of coordinates." His "only" is a tiny speck, like a star.

Yet with understanding and imagination we realize that the "only," like a star, is incomparably vast, impossibly bright. Hotter than hot, farther than far. Not even perhaps, there at all.

○ ○ ○

The rosebush in the front garden I walk past on Albemarle Road in Brooklyn — urban, domestic — was probably planted but is not maintained. This is no English garden. The branches go wild. Children passing by are warned of the thorns creeping over the gate over the narrow sidewalk. It looks spontaneous, exploding there as if by accident. It looks inevitable, too, that rose bush where there needs a burst of color, wild and refined at once in this wild and refined spot. Of course, a rose, of course, a sudden spot of beauty — it is. Blooming with its inevitable arrogance, its generosity, its surprising thorns.

Martha Graham asked about how to reconcile spontaneity with inevitability. The spontaneous happening or done in a natural, often sudden way, without planning or without being forced. The inevitable is certain to happen. Much of life is a dance, mixing these two, making what is done with planning seem spontaneous, what happens without force feels certain to happen. The well-trained dancer's grace reaching over the gate of the garden, exploding color over passersby.

○ ○ ○

Physicists observe that the observer affects the reality. Common sense confirmed by elaborate computation.

○ ○ ○

and

The rain falls
That had not been falling
And it is the same world.

George Oppen from *Of Being Numerous*

○ ○ ○

So much of the world — the world we create by perceiving, as
Merleau-Ponty put it — is dense with feeling, thick with hard
memories, that I look far less often to the neat poem for that hard
feeling of memory-moment to swallow me as I swallow it. All day long
I'm swallowing; it's part of being alive. Poetry attempts to say it.

Still the words surprising on the page are there and come when I turn
to them, with focus. Did I have better focus before? Before Zoom,
before rent, when Abby and I dined on cafeteria food and swapped
stories about professors. When we hung our art on walls with tape
and kept secret babyish comforts still tucked under our pillows. I
made a slow photocopy of Tsvetaeva's poem leaning over the hum of
the large gray machine. Is today's more diffuse looking a dulling vision
or an increasing density of memories cluttering, pressing in? It's never
an either-or when questions are about perception or how I make
sense of the world, how I create my world, ours. It's always both-and,

varying intensities in a more or less forgiving simultaneity.

We used to talk about poetry, but no one can train you to read a poem, only some might give you permission to give the poem your attention. Permission to let this knowledge in, as it comes, without the limits that reduce it. A poetic knowing could come, too, from examining the rug at your feet, the table against your hand, the words uttered by the shopkeeper as you hand over your money. You hand it over. Attending to your own mind is a simultaneity of poetic knowing. Simultaneity of the physicists and poets.

You must be doing something else while sitting. Dragging the pen across the page. Leaning back slightly in the seat. Stepping over a protruding crack in the curb. All simultaneity. And the before returns, happening again. You read this and a remembered sidewalk returns. What do you know about cracks? About stepping? How that moment changed, just now.

o o o

On the streets on the afternoon of the eclipse, neighbors shared their home-made protective glasses, so we all might look toward the cosmos without being blinded, without being permanently damaged by the light.

o o o

Mathematics is abstract even if the proofs add up, the knowing of the numbers is nearly always imaginary. But the abstract depends on these real things. What we touch. What we count. How many words, letters, and how wide the spaces dividing the   ?

When reading about the wars, we are impressed when the soldier stops to read, is able to compose a poem, anything beyond a letter, and even this is precious, surprising, swollen with meaning. Makes an impression.

"The task is to see the riddle."

o o o

Reflecting on the challenges of the biologist conducting physical research, physicist Niels Bohr, in 1932, observed, "In every experiment on living organisms there must remain some uncertainty as regards the physical conditions to which they are subjected, and the idea suggests itself that the minimal freedom we must allow the organism will be just large enough to permit it, so to say, to hide its ultimate secrets from us." Getting to the core without interference of all the conditions that may be touching that core, each atom about which Bohr is curious, remains a mystery.

The mystery provokes more investigations, even as secrets continue to hide. Mysteries becoming smaller, more precise. We become intimate with the world. With each other.

○ ○ ○

Not only to seek knowledge's vague limits, but what might some
understanding or mere thinking of those vast, messy, luminous limits
make way for in the living we do with each other? We trace lines from
A to B but in the entangled bubbling, which clings, spreads, pops, all
of it, in the very metaphor — part of every communication of thought,
the metaphor — is evidence of the limits and the entanglement that
says: wait, pause, care.

To be something and nothing at once, we might imagine the electron:
behaving as a wave and as a particle. To hold this in the mind, the
notion that what is somewhere is not there or it is not possible to
locate it in the way I locate my glasses, here. My phone, my fingernail.
Yet it is making up these things.

Recognize this detached connection as we have questioned the world,
perhaps in youth, head upon my comforting pillow, perhaps yesterday,
walking alone under fluorescent lights at leisure. As we notice the
things we never see: How the skin on the hand up close forms shapes
like triangles. How the song overhead enters our consciousness only
in parts, even though it is, we suspect, playing continuously.

And this particular song takes me to a memory, an unfixed memory,
a sense of my own body in a green place, in a car, lost and singing. I'm
singing in a car and walking through aisles under a fluorescent light.
I stop hearing the song. My day changes, hours are slung lower in a

sense of detached loss.

You may not be able to perceive it at all.

I do not see that glorious scent of the roses.

One thing might tug at the possibility of another, and their connection is part of what makes this space between recognition and knowing emerge: if we get fixed on one thing, the others detach, and this instability is a kind of consistency.

But of course.

o o o

Heisenberg observed that we rely on classical language, classical mechanics, to describe the world not because that is what the world is, but because that is the way we know how to describe it. An act of translation. Heisenberg introduced uncertainty as a language of science. This tickles the poet.

o o o

Walking out of the park, past stoops along the shaded sidewalk, I pass books propped up for the taking. Among them, a book subtitled "A Memoir of Twins Separated and Reunited." It is soiled; I don't pick it up.

Just this morning, I have been reading research on twins, what scientists and psychologists attempt to assert but cannot quite pin down about the mind and the body, nature and nurture; the way twins seem to clarify much and little at the same time. Like walking about and finding a book about twins on this very day clarifies and obscures experience and encounter at the very same time.

On the same sidewalk, in front of a different building, another book. It's on how entrepreneurs practice social responsibility and kindness. Reading jargon like "grit" and "empathy" and "maximize," I become curious about the connection to kindness. I pick it up. But it carries little weight. Its lack of heft saddens me, as if it is evaporating.

○ ○ ○

Relativity, uncertainty, simultaneity, a poetics of encounter and a poetics of knowing must fascinate too. Measurements of distance are affected by the motion of objects being put in relation. And, in no arbitrary sense, we are in motion — the fixed quality is fairly illusory. To move my very hand to take the measurement is a motion. In the abstract sense, change is most continuous, and our interactions are affected by all manner of "movements." How we then measure experience shifts. It has appearances and patterns. We can record and share observations, no doubt. But the fascinating instability of what we encounter is not limited to the assessments of the physicists.

Or, as my beloved philosopher puts it, "My moving body makes a difference in the visible world, being part of it; that is why I can steer it through the visible."

o o o

My contributions may be messy, incomplete, scarred, interrupted, broken, soft, weathered, torn, billowing, edged, parsing, little, fleeting, mild, inchoate, fogged, picked, seared, loose, jiggling, fallen. But they will also be sincere. My contributions will be tender with toil.

o o o

And more than things. Hunger makes me weak. Weakness makes me tired. Reading, I drift off, sometimes from this heaviness, sometimes from a lightness.

Nearness to a photo or a letter or a book makes me link with memories — plural, moving. This making creates. Sleep dips in, and the dream-thought takes over. I forget, and the startling awareness of time, of hours and light, shifts, troubles. There is a car groaning some distance away, outside. I should tidy the table. The shape of the shadow looks like a feather. Or a leg. I forgot to respond to an email. The second hand reaches the twelve. What is the crunching noise? A worker outside? I'm exhausted and writing. It is warm. What near simultaneity is this? Add hunger, add thirst. Add a too-snug shirt or a gust of wind, an odor. Add the call from mother. Add some debt collector.

We can look at the formula for the odor of violets, but the smell will not be on the page, nor the memories conjured when we inhale. We can't even see the odor captured by the scientist, even as it envelopes us when we approach the flower.

Even exhausted, the thoughts are from many directions and touched by time, light, temperature, and other things.

Things. Ten cherries in a bowl. Have I ever even seen a cherry tree? Some would measure the delight, the taste. This measuring is only part of what we know, and this only part of what might become known.

Where does love come in? Whence this fear? The anxiety about corrupt government? The missed deadline and the ominous knock at the door? The last chance? The abandonment? The knowing that death, maybe, death just now or imminent. Loss. So much love emerging as that shadow shifts into the shape of a longer feather, a wing, a falcon.

○ ○ ○

I don't recall reading Einstein. For many years, for my whole life until now. I knew his face. I recognized his famous equation. The t-shirts, the posters. At some point, I knew how to calculate energy, how it was used, as a measurement, as a prediction, what I now think of as a visioning.

What of his words were nevertheless mixed with mine? What did I argue for and against, not hearing with whose ideas I was grappling? Which part of the long debates, sometimes in wooden chairs, sometimes at podiums, did I join, did I take part in, never invited, never heard?

o   o   o

How does it feel to discover something that becomes a killing machine, a weapon of mass — truly massive — destruction? The nuclear bomb. What madness are we celebrating in the image of the mad scientist, head as if on fire?

o   o   o

Reality in science is in part its recognition, over and over in the literature and in the life of the laboratory, of the shifting site of knowledge, of known. The unknown is the curiosity of the scientist — suspicions of hypothesis, wonder of thesis — and not the known, the stuck. Every discovery leads to new questions. These questions do not trouble the reality of science, but rather affirm it. To fix knowledge in place, is, after all, a fiction, a fantasy. Not science. Yet this tension is important. We can know evolution without knowing its cause. We can see or surmise patterns, trajectories, expectations, and build entire worlds on these. This building does not close the questions. The knowing of how does not disclose a why each time. We can understand more and more about larger and ever-smaller increments of experience, and still the unknown expands. Hence the possibility of science coexisting with faith or speculative theological curiosity. Hence the disjunction between strict, limited doctrine and the wonders of scientific learning.

○ ○ ○

"I would have learned so much more if I'd admitted I don't know things."

○ ○ ○

Einstein, putting "truth" in quotation marks, begins the discussion of relativity with the unresolvable concerns — what cannot be measured by geometry's methods, what the limits are of how we can measure the world. Einstein asks us to attend to the ways we assume that what we know — the Euclidean geometry measuring a straight line between two points — is relative, is unstable, is a study in how very uncertain our ways of claiming truth are.

To know where one object is located, Einstein continues, we must locate it in relation to something else. This is where the measurements begin, to start with a point and extend to another, with numbers marking the in-between. But this also is where we might begin to wobble, to shake, as the certainty of the one is dependent on the other, and we ourselves are in relation to these. The cloud moving in as we find it.

○ ○ ○

I hike to the top of a mountain near the Cilento in Italy and below I see orange rooftops. The earth appears to be a flattish plane covered with buildings, here rising and falling, here spreading with water or swelling with soil, blurring under dust. I live understanding that my proximity to the streets changes them. The town that has swallowed me like a stifling gas now is tiny, harmless, charming. The clouds cast their shadows, but only here and there — shapes shifting as the wind and the sun's rays shift. The valley becomes small.

Another afternoon, I decide to walk home, across Brooklyn, rather than take the subway so many stops. The distance is the same, the time stretches, but the earth becomes smaller, more intimate, mine to traverse. A different kind of smallness.

○ ○ ○

Einstein writes "Every description of events in space involves the use of a rigid body to which such events have to be referred. The resulting relationship takes for granted that the laws of Euclidean geometry hold for 'distances,' the 'distance' being represented physically by means of the convention of two marks on a rigid body."

The living body is not rigid. The conventions Einstein asks us to puzzle over are the conventions of a dead nothing — where the entangled world is mystically transfigured into a disentangled

Euclidean track of straight line from point to point. Even the bird is stillness. Yet, and he tells us, there is nothing quite "true" in this figure that disentangles for the sake of the convention. For the sake of reasoning the dead. Even the rare mustached kingfisher, captured and stored in the American Museum of Natural History, truly dead, is a link to the life of the bird, the South Pacific, the radiant color of the forest.

The living are not rigid bodies yet. Even the things we observe are nothing but things-in-relation. Are nothing, are but things, are in relation, all three at once.

On Entangling Threads

> Remembering and forgetting are functions of a brain, but
> there is no memory or forgetting without a past, no memory
> or forgetting without others in that past, and those memories
> are consolidated in the brain by emotion, and my emotions also
> have a history that affects how I feel now.

> Siri Hustvedt, *A Woman Looking at Men
> Looking at Women: Essays on Sex, Art and
> the Mind*

There weren't enough to choose from: not enough eagles
overhead, swooping, not enough majestic forests, not enough
majesty. I've been looking for what to tell of history, of love.
There aren't enough of it, or any.

Only stone signposts, overgrown with weeds.
Still, the old stone signposts overgrown with weeds.

o o o

In ancient times, followers of Pythagoras ascribed their own
discoveries to him, enhancing his reputation, blurring out the

community of learning that sprawled, intersecting. The tidying of this history into one man's name dilutes our understanding, implies a kind of learning at odds with what really happens and how we really come to know and revise knowing. Claiming a cohesive narrative is this mistake.

"Most [American] founders could not imagine a society where women were free and equal and were governed by their own consent. They usually wrote and spoke about freedom, equality, and consent in politics as if women did not exist." This insight is observed by Mark E. Kann in *The Gendering of American Politics,* a book in the shadowy shelves of the library. After reading this passage, I sit a long while looking out a tall, old window in a monumental, old building, then go out for fresh air in the city park. In the busy park at lunchtime, one feels rather invisible.

Recognition is comfort for those who control the situation. Routine can comfort those who are controlled. What patterns emerge from comforts outside controlling hierarchies?

In "The Subjection of Women," John Stuart Mill argued that because they benefit from the subservience of women, men "enslave the minds" of women by bringing them up to believe they are opposite of men — it is "artificial."

This was in 1869.

In thinking of the eagles, swooping, the mind already changes — you begin to think of ways you can and do alter your experience. Baldwin tells us that to change how we see the world is to change the world. Some changes feel forced upon us. Imagine that sudden rain-shower that dampened your shoulders. You didn't choose it. We know, we are shaped by our encounters. Some we choose. Others are artificial.

○ ○ ○

I felt angry when a boy aggressively sprayed me with a fierce hose in the hot backyard. What should I do but run away or stand in the sun letting my shirt dry? And the story becomes "kids playing in the yard."

○ ○ ○

The reach for a proof of experience frustrates the thinker. You, me. Attempting to put into language this notion is frustrating. The proof itself — of being alive, of having awareness of experience, of Being itself in the complex and indeterminate philosophical sense — slips, a moving target. The frustration is multifold, first in its dependence on language, a notoriously disappointing aspect of that experience. The thinker who puts into language this thought about experience immediately has an impact on the encounter itself, and thus the language too becomes altered.

The teacher wrote in gooey blue ink: *be more specific.* The subtext: you're being obtuse. The problem: I want to think about what it all means, not a passing grade. Then I write: *be more specific* in clattering keystrokes.

There is no telling of an experience that is not experienced as a telling. And the listening or reading is experienced, too, and then those finicky words get rolled back on, lose their fixity, alter themselves. Even on the printed page, the language is undone from its thinking into words, undone from one experience to another, thought to written thought, and even that first thought is destabilized again. The unhinged is unhinging.

To read the word is to interact with it too, as writer or as distant reader, opening a dusty book or clicking on a blinking screen. And that dust, it alters those words a bit as you read them. You rub your eyes, you slow down. The blinking screen, it makes demands on you that frustrate your attention. You experience all this. The thought, the thought about experience itself, it is experienced. Where it goes, has been, will be, is always entangled, and as each effort to isolate it emerges, so too a new intersection. The isolation is impossible, even if its effort is endlessly productive of new intersections, new entanglements, given the attention to pursue then as idea. Knowledge is not static.

o o o

Knowing love changes love. Thinking love alters what you know of it.

○ ○ ○

"For Husserl, this ability to describe a phenomenon without influence from others' theories is what liberates the philosopher," Sarah Bakewell tells us. It is a curious idea, given the way philosophers rely on other philosophers to explain their work. Edmund Husserl attempted to move closer to encounter, to description. He is called the founder of phenomenology. What can we learn by studying all the things around us and ourselves and others?

There is no way to distinguish the world from the interactions that constitute it — and how it matters, becomes matter and meaning. "The world is intra-activity in its differential mattering," writes physicist Karen Barad. The interactive becomes an exchange, intertwines, intra-action.

That rainy day did not only happen to us. We interacted with it,
        intra-acting.
The biting spray of the hose hurt then; is still hurting.

Soaked, not in peace.
Life, liberty, and.

○ ○ ○

Each person has a private archive: those works we've discovered and remembered, the readings we keep close and that keep us, ropes of thought holding us captive and reaching beyond what we actively remember. Our private archives are our evidence of entanglement. How we have understood the poetic mind has been echoed in the scientific vocabulary of matter and energy. And so, the thinking, the philosophical mind unhinged from rigid requirements of patriarchal lineage of Western thought, might be better understood outside the confines of old reason.

"Phenomena are produced through agential intra-actions of multiple apparatuses of bodily production." This is, again, Barad. I slow down, close my eyes and open at each word. What does it mean, phenomena? What does it mean agential? We make stuff happen, but it's more than that. It's everything. It's touch and vision. I'm looking at everything. It's also mind, also memory. It's what never happened. Phenomena are produced.

I was in St. Petersburg, Russia, and I wrote in my journal:

> *On the metro today I rode with such*
> *searching eyes ... looking, searching*
> *for "him" — either the one I missed*
> *or the one I always miss.*

I had just turned twenty-one.

o o o

In quantum physics, the philosophical and the physical turn toward each other in interdisciplinarity as a necessary clarification. Science always demanded that language communicate its meanings, often metaphorically, but here the language had to stretch to imagine its worlds and experiments, too.

The problems of a linear, sequential, certain vision of the knowable become obvious. Such an expectation of knowledge leads to oppression. It apologizes for delays in granting humanity based on excuses of history and readiness, the excuses of the timeline, of the logic of change. Patriarchy is perpetuated because tradition and the limits are not only recognized but celebrated as progress.

○ ○ ○

In Book II of Plato's *Republic*, Glaucon conflates the question of justice — what does it mean to be just? do we even value justice for its own sake? — with the power to evade punishment for injustice or to be powerful enough to enjoy the privilege of choosing injustice. The story of the ring of invisibility, which the shepherd finds and uses to seduce the queen, slay the king, and take over the kingdom, is used as "evidence" that people would choose injustice if immunity came with it. I don't find the reasoning persuasive. The assumptions undergirding the logic are cruel, aggressive, and foreign to much experience — though not foreign to legend or myth or the rhetoric of the state. Invisible, might he not approach each bed and tuck the covers around lonely bodies more warmly? Invisible, might we not move food to the hand of the hungry?

If the myths repeat violence and we attend to them, what are we reinscribing? Assumptions of brutality are embedded within celebrated texts exalted for their intimacy with notions of the true.

What if we assumed love first, how would all of Western philosophy be altered?

○ ○ ○

The "Lady of Little Faith" asks about love, how to reconcile loving humanity with loving individuals, and whether it is possible to live with this challenge not in despair. "No," Father Zosima tells her. One must not despair. But yes, distress is a necessary part of it. "Love in dreams is greedy for immediate action, rapidly performed and in sight of all," Dostoevsky writes. "But active love is labor and fortitude and for some people, too, perhaps a complete science." Faith can assert love in multiple directions at once: love of the divine, and divine love, for us and for others, and our own capacity — in faith—for loving beyond ourselves. Simone Weil says loving ourselves, too, is part of this faith — perhaps the most difficult.

To define one thing against another is startling, prescriptive, limiting, circumscribing, oppressive, banal. That this world ever makes sense is as startling as defining blue as not-yellow, blue as not-round. It is accurate — blue is not yellow — but not definitive.

○ ○ ○

If the physicist can imagine a continuum in which time stretches and compresses, in which what I do now and what happens elsewhere overlap in ways that are unrecognizable to the experience I describe as my "everyday" living, then can't the imagination stretch to reach a different dimension of meaningful ethics, working to not only understand but insist on the possibility and necessity of the good? And in this work insisting, too, on the living of it — that we might both think about ethics and be living transformed by the thinking? There are other ways of knowing and other values we may already even hold but fail to recognize — informed by religion, oppression, empathy, racism, patriarchy, possibility, family, and the challenges of freedom and of love.

o o o

I hear a goose flying by. It makes a sound in the air — its voice a doubling squawk. Who imagined it flying? On the ground, it lumbers. On the ground, ungainly. I must never have seen the moment it stopped being grounded and became a bird in flight. I measure something against this failure to see or imagine. I measure many spaces I fail to see or imagine. The sound is long gone.

And to see the body would have meant nothing.

o o o

The apparatuses we use to understand the world are open-ended practices, they have indeterminacy. In physics.

What are we paying attention to?

I cannot move with the dancer's body's grace. The stretch of the tendons is an impossibility. Her arm outstretched so the skin beneath it is taut, the air reaching those hidden parts. Yet the tilt of the head over the curved neck feels familiar.

Still my neck moves altogether differently, like so.

The dancer's body captures mine as I see it moving, and my body is detached from my bent seated figure, this stiff form, detached from its immobility even as it sits, the eye alone following the dance.

As the apparatuses are "open-ended practices," characterized by indeterminacy, we too are indeterminate. Our interactions are experiences which shape us and each other, are also not fixed. We move in time and are altered, as we too are altering, not only on a forward-moving progressive linear trajectory, but also in other directions, changing our memories, remapping ourselves, and altering others. The triviality of small comfort in a sense of fixed narrative of a life or history or relationship is a false wisdom when we apply it to our intimate lives, is an even grosser distortion when applied to history or to abstract intellectual projects. To imagine that moving forward on the same-old-line of progressing thought is itself change, linear motion as change does not clarify how we know or understand. The trajectory shows we age but does not clarify newly what might have been long in shadow.

Tucked in my heavy desk drawer I find a poem I composed decades ago. Or part of a poem. Before I fell in and out of love and back in again, I wrote the poem and called it "Twelve."

> A deck of cards is summer by a lake
> > in New Hampshire, with rain veiling
> > our tiny cabin, with
> Time on our hands.
>
> Lilacs are the last walk home
> > from the bus stop in junior high, June
> > maybe, and sand crunching beneath my feet.
> Walking down the little hill, the curve
> > before the house, loving
> > the smell of lilacs, imagining
> Escaping youth.

We can measure the distance the dancer's arm moves, but not the grace of it. We can imagine becoming older, blowing out candles for every year we reach, but not the moment we reach today, ourselves, becoming. Wasn't I always noticing the crunch of earth underfoot? And yesterday, I watched my daughter marvel at the wet crackling ice on pavement, opening up to puddles underneath.

○ ○ ○

The trajectory shows we age but does not clarify newly what might
have been long in shadow. Sometimes established definitions establish
subordination, as where the feminine is not understood outside its
relation to masculine, whereas masculinity or the masculine itself is a
definition, a thing, its own understanding. What does it mean to seek
meanings? Is most philosophy a justification for oppression
and violence?

○ ○ ○

Interrupted by your arrival, it startles me, glittering
with life, but away from the book, the pen, these quicker comforts.
The slow ink will be here for me. I will need it again, and it will wait.

This, our time, which I eagerly stand to meet, greet, to enjoy, this
our time that might please struggle for decades — might please long
and glittering — all the time we might enjoy will not, like the pen, wait.

○ ○ ○

"Intra-actions always entail particular exclusions, and exclusions
foreclose any possibility of determinism, providing the condition of
an open future." They invite us to imagine differently. "Therefore,
intra-actions are constraining but not determining. That is, intra-
activity is neither a matter of strict determinism nor unconstrained

freedom." What do I remember? What happened? Who did I miss on that Russian metro so many years ago? What's changed now that I'm remembering. I read my own journal and times slips. "The future is radically open at every turn."

Constraining but not determining.
And at the same time, simultaneity clarified by quantum mechanics.

○ ○ ○

We open and open as we are opening. There is a looking back and forward as we are acted upon and acting. James Baldwin, to be specific, wrote: "The world changes according to the way people see it, and if you alter, even but a millimeter the way people look at reality, then you can change it." This is the writer's work, but also this is living.

Live responsibly.
"Be specific." It's true and untrue at once. Important and impossible.

Not unlike the lost letter, discovered after many years in a drawer or tucked away in a trunk, the reading of a work by more readers, more of us, changes its relation to the world and the world's relation to it. The letter's discovery makes it a different piece of paper. Its reading makes the reader's mind and relation to its writer change. This is true even if the letter is read by its own writer, as in rediscovering one's own old diary.

Even the simplest math is imprecise. Two large apples plus two larger apples make a different four, although they are the same quantity. We are still counting. The meaning of four might change, grow, and become more precise. What is understood as fixed knowledge becomes loosened for potential discovery, re-evaluation, and imminent learning. The tiny cabin in the rain. I found it tucked in a drawer.

○ ○ ○

We are adept at, trained in, expert in the scroll, the skim. To skim the surface and assess swiftly the necessary, the basic, the only-what-is-needed is a practice for the overapplied student and the bored worker, the consumer. We can skim, it serves us when too much is presented. We skim headlines, we scroll to evaluate the oversaturation of information: calorie counts, movie titles, even the news stories we might decide to consume, even our friends' lives become skimmable, "posts" to pick and choose rather than connections to make, people to get to know, problems to unravel and problems to study.

The poet develops a deep respect for the technical work in fundamental physics. Entering a book, another book, a third, the language of theoretical physics is like the vocabulary of a foreigner never able to travel to the land of native speakers, tongue full of awkwardness. Still, the love for the language is sincere, if budding, and the efforts to improve her accent ongoing. The native speaker may find it hard to decipher the stumbling utterance — as if yet a new poethysics emerges, lisping.

One of my students struggles with pronouncing *sh* and *ch* sounds in new words. *We do not have this in Arabic,* she explains. Still, she speaks, she learns the differences.

Simultaneity makes emergent experience possible. The limitations of the categorical, the ranking, even the naming itself — language's very doing and being — undermines the understanding that comes when simultaneity of, for example, metaphorical (poetics) and symbolic (art) thinking suggests reality, allowing both recognition and even beloved empathy, which is a simultaneity of both recognition and otherness. Long have writers and thinkers and artists and *the wise* recognized the importance of complexity in sophisticated thought, that simplicity is often deceptive. To see the simple at all — to recognize it as such — is to acknowledge it against complexity, ever in relation, as simultaneity demands.

Even without the sounds, my student can say *wish* and *share.* She can say, *She chooses.*

o o o

If knowing comes in a sequence, then make a list. Cloud, rain, puddle, or puddle, pool, pond, ocean, or bodies in the ocean. Knowing fractures. The work of making an embodied study that also attends to knowledge, the matter of being, and being itself, and transcends while remaining of this experience, not deciding between material and immaterial, but navigating the strangeness of the relationship between these, and that the complexities of those relations unfurl into not a this and a that (material, immaterial) but an entangled live, changing, interconnected, and impenetrable but sensible something. In this list language is insufficient, just as any one single item is insufficient in apprehending the collection.

Even experience is a messy list: we see, but we see textures, distances, feel things. We hear, but sound too is the feeling world. We do not separate these. To smell is to taste and memory entangles. Touch feels isolated sometimes (feels!) but betrays itself to be dependent on space in a way that links with our other senses.

Encounter a work of art differently, be a slower reader of all things exposing some legibility — books, news, images, each other, the very spaces they inhabit — but from that attention, its practice and reflection, encounters continue, and the core of engagement emerges, the unexamined life dissipates.

Knowledge is not static.

o o o

The mind, yet it alters, but the flesh — the hand that might touch your skin and remember its feeling, the eye that lingers on your body alongside mine as this hand moves

on yours, and your hair, your body — these things don't
wait like the paper. The mind needs its changes,
its memories, to be made. We are in the making time.

o o o

Threads come together, with some care, string by string, over and
over, drawn through. We bring together the piece until a new one
emerges — blanket, tapestry, braid.

o o o

The loving attention is both a leaning into the thing of the world
and a moving away from it. We can't be fully with another and
generously give loving attention. This awareness informs, shapes
some of the (sometimes beautiful) heartache we associate with love,
the recognition of this necessary distance between ourselves and the
beloved, between I and you, my love, that is as tender and loving as
is made possible by my sensing the distance that we can't close. The
loving attention is not a self-gratifying one. It hurts, even as it extends
our attention, a suffering.

*Choosing to continue to make — love and memories, the small
majesties. Take my hand. Then the pen, waiting, will find its time,
its words. And we look up and notice the goose flying, one with other
geese, and they are together creating a shape in the sky. The air
pressed by wings into unknown gusts of wind.*

Thread: *We are always in ruins*

> The hidden life of love is in the most inward depths,
> unfathomable, and still has an unfathomable relationship with
> the whole of existence.
>
> > Søren Kierkegaard, *Works of Love*

We might think the numbers are just smarter than we are, that maybe
we just haven't figured out the proof yet. We have figured out that
there are many proofs.

We shape the world in many ways: roads, homes, meals. We shape
how we see with paint and clay, framing the vistas. We shape
understanding too.

We weave the threads into fabric, stitch fabric into clothing, wear it.

In Pompeii, we find painted walls, broken stone staircases, carved
columns, vast rooms shaped by walls patterned in stone and tile,
color and texture. Two thousand years ago this was long achieved
and destroyed.

Logics multiply. We understand this to be both an idea, as in a thought of language, and mathematics. The mathematician understands much about abstraction. To have an idea of the number is to think beyond counting things and to extend ideas to thoughts beyond language of words, too. The mathematician seeks proofs, but the more the mathematician seeks the more the proofs, too, multiply. There are many paths to some answers. And some answers feel like magic.

Shapes can be more than the square or the circle. Measure, measure again, and the measuring makes another line. Shapes can shift, be altered, be mistaken, be metamorphosized. Even our bodies change. We shape understanding too. "[T]here is no such thing as an independently existing trajectory, but only a trajectory relative to a trajectory relative to a particular body of relation."

Mythologies make something possible. What makes it possible to create peace?

I pause at a crossroads as the sun sets over Pompeii. I squint over stones, turn to see the distant mountain. "Look," I say to my small family.

The linear narrative oppresses by assuming a conformity that does not correspond with experience, then makes the body work to conform to it in order to make sense of the linearity ("in order"). This training is from without and from within. This training is not in one part of the experience — the body with a shape, a texture, an age, its details we name as gender, race, the aging body, the able body, the transgressive body in its many potential ways. We recognize transgression as part of the linear narrative. It zigzags.

In Pompeii, what did the women do, looking up to the ceiling where bodies of women were carved, diaphanous robes carved in stone, holding instruments and weapons, hair ornately braided? We learn, we forget, knowing and not knowing. What did they ponder, stepping out of the room between the carved columns before the lava poured? This, we do not know.

Like memory, what comes and goes and is here and gone at once, so too experience. I am holding this pen and not holding it. You are reading and simultaneously other verbs are defining your now. Remember and recall, slipping away and holding fast, here and not here. Your eye moves from word to word — it is a line telling me about its shape — but what happened when you blinked? Did the line continue? The steadfastness of continuity is so strange a story, I wonder how it holds so tight. What's "winning"? That hurts.

I visit Pompeii and get disoriented by the stones. The roofless walls make the sky swallow all direction. I feel lost and time insists on our finding direction. We all have to get out, find our way before closing time. The sun is setting. A great change. The sky is dimming.

Greatness matters: the way the great intersects with strength, power, dominance, and fear, and its awkward relation to the intersection of great and good. We say, in casual chatter, that these are synonyms; it's great, super, good. But greatness is also the history of a dark shadow of Peter the Great, Gilgamesh, Odysseus, the fighters whom we have called heroes. Great men, what have they done? Greatness is ominous, too, in its diminishment of the good. If all would be good, and less great, this would be, rather, super.

The guide-book tells me, in a small dwelling in the north part of the site, tourists can see plaster casts of an entire family. "The striking aspect of the house is the discovery of the bodies of an entire family. The family consisted of masters and servants, although they cannot be distinguished from each other." Their fallen bodies are on display now, but I will not see them. We are late. The sun is setting. Soon darkness will blanket the site.

"How does it all begin?" asked Martha Graham. "I suppose it never begins. It just continues," she answered.

Mythology silences, and our own story might be a circle, pretending to be fractal. It is not a matter of forgetting. This trajectory is a matter of relation.

The place doesn't demand its way of arrival. Yet there it is. This may, too, be love. How it arrives and exists and thrives and changes us is a matter of relation. We do recognize love, name its hows and whys, its many ways of finding and being. And still there it is, a shock of love.

My heart, breaking with the family's frozen bodies that I don't have time to see.

How does it all begin? I suppose it never begins. It just continues.

Pain, too, comes. It goes. Imagine if it didn't go? It is some learning we need: pain's winding path. The sky is so beautiful.
The ocean.

Seeking a path to exit, I feel lost among the ruins, even with our map. All the stones start to look alike, massive and gray. Where was the room with the carvings? Where was the ceiling with the woman's body behind a flowing sheet of cloth, stiff in tile? Lost.

When great meant, at some other juncture, big, massive, and coarse, great was large. Great-big. Grosse. Be large and be great; be small and diminished. Force becomes celebrated not just for size, but in value, great and good. These myths become the truths, this "truth" becomes religion, these become how we decide and live and behave. And what if these become how we love, diluting it from its thick heat, its lava.

"We have found the Indians very faithful in their Covenant of Peace with us; very loving and ready to pleasure us. We often go to them; and they come to us. Some of us have been fifty miles by land in the country with them," reported by Mourt and published in 1622.

I grew up near Salem. I visit Pompeii.

The myths shape us even when we acknowledge them as fiction. *No more masks! No more mythologies!* Acknowledge what happened and all the ways in which we oppress and fail and love. Other words, refusal of myth. Other words, other ways.

There is no such thing as an independently existing trajectory.

A reported 22 people died in the arena, walking out of the concert the night it was bombed. Young girls were dancing, then the explosion.

After returning from Italy, I visit Green-Wood Cemetery, where some gravesites are large stately stones inscribed with surnames: Holmes, Kraemer, Sommer. Before the large stones are set smaller ones. Many read MOTHER on top. Next to MOTHER is FATHER. Next to MOTHER is DAUGHTER.

Some words are there for something beyond understanding. A reported 276 girls were forced from their school, forced, and forced. As years pass, girls become women. What is it to be a woman? What do we call the missing people, if we do not call them by name?

Grasp relativity, loosen knowing to emerge toward ethical wisdom, weave stories anew and anew. Attend to those we have missed, pressing up so close.

MOTHER lived from 1868 until 1936: 68 years. Nearby GEORGE lived from 1894 until 1901.

In 68 years, we do much more than to mother.

Some paths in the cemetery are more mysterious than others. More covered in shade, with graves less frequently looked upon. Grass grows unmown. Stone edges soften under weather.

Alongside MOTHER and GEORGE, the gravesites of other children. Some live more than 7 years.

Minnie Cohen collected all the inscriptions from all the stones in a series of books. The books are fragile, old, typed on yellowing paper.

Retreat, not into silence, but contemplation that would become something else, a reaching. It takes patience to track threads entangling.

Today, another mother dies. She is a poet. She is a lover, daughter, traveler, drinker of coffee and drinker of tea, my friend. Patient and impatient, she is a piece of memory and of life.

After the visit to the cemetery, after the visit to the ruins, after the memorial service, after the poem is written and the poem is read, after the hand outstretched draws the gate closed and the heavy weight of its lock clatters, here at the gate the unseen bodies follow, the unmet friend laughs. The gates close but the great entanglement opens wider. A new beloved teacher finds me through a book written years before I was born, and I am changed.

Further Entanglements, Works Cited, End Notes

Notes pages 11 – 18

Heraclitus. *Fragments*, trans. Brooks Haxton, et al. (New York: Penguin Classics, 2003), 7.

> Begin with a piece from *Fragments*. It is not arbitrary.

Martha Graham. *Blood Memory: An Autobiography* (New York: Doubleday, 1991), 17.

> Filled with photographs and anecdotes, bits of letters and remembered conversations, yet little Graham writes comes close to the power of Graham's own body in motion, the dancer. The book is also a kind of auto-memorial, written even as she was about to die. The body of a dancer trying to find its way into language.

Stacy Schiff. *The Witches: Suspicion, Betrayal, and Hysteria in 1692 Salem* (New York: Little, Brown, 2015).

> Suspicion emerges from a knowing that comes from hints, clues, incomplete information. The hunch shrouded in ominousness. Often awareness comes first as suspicion. The title points us to suspicion.

The New England Primer, originally published in 1777 by Edward Draper, adapted and sold in reproduction by Clippership Publications, 2001.

> The reproduction is a tiny booklet. I wonder how large it was when printed in 1777, and a quick search for the original

reveals that the booklet was tiny in 1777, too, 80 bound pages. Small enough to fit in a small hand.

Brooklyn Museum of Art https://www.brooklynmuseum.org/exhibitions/cecilia_vicuna

Later, in 2022, I see different hanging knotted works by Vicuña at the Guggenheim Museum in New York. I think of these as a poetry of form, different from the quipus I saw at the Brooklyn Museum, harder to decipher.

Michelle Boulous Walker. *Slow Philosophy: Reading against the Institution* (New York: Bloomsbury, 2016), 57.

There are many thrills in this book, but to share just one, on page 4: "Calculative thinking involves a flight from thinking, a total thoughtlessness that reduces all to system and calculated intention. [...] It is a kind of thinking incapable of contemplation." See also page 61.

Niels Bohr. *Atomic Physics and Human Knowledge* (Mineola: Dover, 1961, 2010).

Barad discusses Bohr, too, as an inspiration and influence, which is reassuring.

Yiannis Ritsos. *Exile & Return: Selected Poems* 1967-1974, trans. Edmund Keeley (New York: Ecco, 1985; repr. 1987, 1989).

During different periods of his life, Ritsos spent years in various prisons and later under house arrest as a political prisoner, yet some online searches only mention that he was "arrested." Strange word choice, this erasure of imprisonment. One site says he was "exiled to a prison camp," an opaque verb to describe captivity.

John Milton. *Paradise Lost.* Penguin Classics 2003.

I'm puzzled by citation practices that don't reveal the original date of publication. We should know, at a glance, that Paradise Lost was published in 1667 and again in 1674 with revisions, but standard references in 2022 don't require either of these details.

Mary Beth Norton. *In the Devil's Snare: The Salem Witchcraft Crisis of 1692.* Vintage 2003.

The lecture I listened to informs, or is informed by, this book.

Laurel Thatcher Ulrich. *Good Wives: Image and Reality in the Lives of Women in Northern New England,* 1650-1750 (New York: Alfred A. Knopf, 1982, Vintage, 1991).

This curious title evokes not only good and evil but the culture familiar through the "Goodman" title for average folk like the Massachusetts characters in Hawthorne's historical tales and recalling the phrase "good book" as synonym for the Bible. No wonder I'm such a slow reader, dwelling over titles as if they are poems.

Rebecca Solnit. *Men Explain Things To Me.* (Haymarket, 2014)

Each chapter begins with a photograph, and in "Grandmother Spider," a beloved essay, she weaves images of fabrics, textiles, and the women tending them, with history and current events, to explore the troubling tradition of women's erasure, obliteration, and disappearance.

Fernando Pessoa. "The Keeper of Sheep." *A Little Larger Than the Entire Universe: Selected Poems,* trans. Richard Zenith (New York: Penguin 2006), 12.

Seeing oneself as a "medium," as Pessoa put it, evokes something seductive and possibly liberating about publishing under different names, There are other names·to list when writing about Pessoa. Fernando Pessoa and Alberto Caeiro, one of his "heteronyms," and even the translator, Richard Zenith, whose composition of the poems I read in this selection.

Søren Kierkegaard. *Works of Love,* trans. Howard and Edna Hong (New York: Harper, 1962), 23.

My paperback copy of this book is inscribed with my former last name and my college dorm room telephone extension.

Marina Tsvetaeva. *Selected Poems,* trans. Elaine Feinstein (New York: Penguin, 1971, 1993), 11.

In notes, it says this poem is "addressed to Mandelstam." Another entanglement.

Marguerite Duras. *Writing,* trans. Mark Polizzotti (Cambridge:

Lumen, 1993, 1998).

I draw from the section called "Wartime Writings" I wonder if it's possible to read all Duras' works as wartime writing, every line describing her adolescence or imagined characters, and even the loving fragments written in *No More (C'est Tout)* at the end of her life.

William Bradford. "Of Plymouth Plantation." *The Mayflower Papers: Selected Writings of Colonial New England* (New York: Penguin, 2007), 13.

This is a speculative moment in Bradford's discussion of Plymouth Plantation, a report on conditions and an imagining of what a future might be. He imagines children looking back on trials of their father's with praise and appreciation.

Marina Tsvetaeva. *Selected Poems,* trans. Elaine Feinstein (New York: Penguin, 1971, 1993), Again.

The copy I have of this book is the very one I held up to the copy machine. A black and white photograph of the poet appears on the cover. Her eyes stare out and her hands are carefully crossed on her lap. She wears rings and bracelets and what appears to be a heavy necklace, but her gaze draws my attention more. On the back cover of the paperback is a note in small font: "Cover photograph: INTERFOTO, Munich." No date.

Simone Weil. *Gravity and Grace,* trans. Emma Crawford and Marion von der Ruhr. (New York: Routledge, 1947, 2002), 62.

Weil often writes about love, directly and indirectly. If I need to reorient myself in relation to love's importance, I open Weil.

Simone Weil. *Gravity and Grace,* trans. Emma Crawford and Marion von der Ruhr. (New York: Routledge, 1947, 2002).

Again, and ongoing. Elsewhere, and for me first, in *Waiting for God* Weil links attention – and attention to studies – to prayer. And then I feel suddenly quite devout.

Ecclesiastes, Bible. New Revised Standard Version Bible (Grand Rapids: Zondervan, 1989)

I look up the word "skeptic" in the Merriam-Webster Dictionary app and find these two definitions: 1. an adherent or advocate of skepticism and 2. a person disposed to skepticism especially regarding religion or religious principles. And "skepticism" is listed as an attitude of doubt or incredulity.

Søren Kierkegaard. *Works of Love,* trans. Howard and Edna Hong (New York: Harper, 1962), 161.

Months after writing these words, this book comes up in casual conversation, and in the din of a restaurant all I can draw to mind is the relationship between "love" and "duty," and this feels like something different than remembering.

Laurel Thatcher Ulrich. *Good Wives: Image and Reality in the Lives of Women in Northern New England, 1650-1750* (New York: Alfred A. Knopf, 1982, Vintage, 1991).

The inequality here is common knowledge, surely, a "suspicion." But also reported in Good Wives.

Theodor Adorno. *Minima Moralia: Reflections from Damaged Life*, trans. E.F.N. Jephcott (London: Verso, 2006), 26.

I have little to say about Adorno except that I came to this book late, and perhaps too late.

bell hooks. *All About Love: New Visions* (New York: Morrow, 2001, 2018), 47.

This book was on the bestseller list for months in 2022, after hooks died in late 2021, 23 years after its original publication.

Roland Barthes. *A Lover's Discourse*, trans. Richard Howard (New York: Hill and Wang, 1979, 2010), 77-78.

The citations in Barthes' book are marginal namings, hints that don't interrupt the text, an inspiration. The first part of this book is entitled "How this book was constructed," and here Barthes writes about the references. He offers a kind of disclaimer: "The references supplied in this fashion are not authoritative but amical: I am not invoking guarantees, merely recalling, by a kind of salute given in passing, what has seduced, convinced, or what has momentarily given the delight of understanding (of being understood?)."

Luce Irigaray. *The Way of Love*, trans. Heidi Bostic and Stephen

Pluhàcek (London: Continuum, 2002), 17.

Reading Irigaray requires intensity and ease, relaxing into its density, its intensity.

Heraclitus. *Fragments*, trans. Brooks Haxton (New York: Penguin Classics, 2003), 11.

A student reminds me of the most famous passage from Heraclitus, that you cannot step in the same stream twice. I remember an earlier moment reading Heraclitus, when I too was a student. In that old textbook fervid underlinings course through every page of the chapter on Heraclitus.

Susan Sontag. "The Aesthetics of Silence." *Styles of Radical Will* (New York: Farrar, Straus and Giroux 1969), 21.

Tucked into the book at the end of this first chapter is a small orange piece of paper with my daughter's name on it in another child's handwriting: "I really liked your message and all your emotion through your poem." I wonder who wrote this and I wonder about the message. Neither of us remember, but the silence of memory is remarkable, too.

Wendy Warren. *New England Bound: Slavery and Colonization in Early America* (New York: Liveright Norton, 2016), 133.

This is the sort of entanglement I might be inclined to avoid, growing up in New England and proud of its abolitionist roots, yet they must necessarily coexist with the roots in slavery.

Luke 6:35 (New Revised Standard Version, 1989)

Occasionally in my adolescence we went to sermons in a church in a small New England town. It was the closest I could get to a philosophical lecture at the time.

Khaled Hosseini, *The Kite Runner* (New York, Riverhead, 2003), 359.

A popular novel.

M. NourbeSe Philip as told to the author by Setaey Adamu Boateng. *Zong!* (Middletown, CT: Wesleyan University Press, 2008).

Two authors, an evocation of ancestry. Ancestry is a thread, if the reader wishes to track it. Zong! offers powerfully visual poetry, drawn from documentary sources, and in the Notanda gives information to more deeply engage with it; a most generous volume, bigger than its 211 pages. Poetry and legal history, guiding and haunted. I've written about this elsewhere.

Svetlana Alexievich. *The Unwomanly Face of War: An Oral History of Women in World War II*, trans. Richard Pevear and Larissa Volokhonsky. (New York: Random House, 2017), xxii. A gathering of voices, Alexievich's writing is sometimes called "polyphonic."

⊘ Jérôme Ferrari. *The Principle,* trans. Howard Curtis. (New York: Europa, 2016), 15.

The principle is uncertainty, or the more we determine the less we can predict. I cannot read the mathematical physics, and Ferrari doesn't include equations in the novel, but the principle is nevertheless a curiosity.

⊘ Michelle Boulous Walker. *Slow Philosophy: Reading Against the Institution* (Bloomsbury: 2015).

I often share this quote with students, and we puzzle together over the "ethical."

⊘ Bergson, Henri. *Creative Evolution,* trans. Arthur Mitchell (New York: Barnes & Noble, 1907, 1911, 2005).

I cannot locate my copy of Bergson's book on my shelf, a frustration that leads me to reflect on its dull cover with its small font and boring orange design, what I remember of the object.

⊘ Wendy Warren. *New England Bound: Slavery and Colonization in Early America* (New York: Liveright Norton, 2016), 33.

A notable chapter by Warren investigates Samuel Sewall's early abolitionist pamphlet The Selling of Joseph: A Memorial. Sewall is the same Sewall who was the only judge to express repentance for his participation in the Salem witch trials. See also Judge Sewall's Apology by Richard Francis (2006). Warren "wonders how Samuel Sewall came to write such radical sentiments in The Selling of Joseph," asking "Was it perhaps, then, his experience with the Salem witchcraft trials?" (243).

Deuteronomy 15:12-17; Corinthians 7:21-24.

The ministers in the congregation of my youth were a red-bearded man and a long-haired woman. My family moved away from that town decades ago.

Luce Irigaray. *The Way of Love,* trans. Heidi Bostic and Stephen Pluhàcek (London: Continuum, 2002), 6.

In the margins of this introduction, I've doodled the unhinged triangle, a figure I drew to capture "the unsayable" in my 2017 book. The image evokes more than the words, sometimes. Later in the book, on page 86, Irigaray writes, "To come back to oneself, after such a movement, does not grant to the subject a simply unity."

Maurice Merleau-Ponty. "Indirect Language and the Voices of Silence", trans. Michael B. Smith. *The Merleau-Ponty Aesthetics Reader.* (Evanston: Northwestern University Press, 1993), 82.

If you follow only one thread, this one.

Luce Irigaray. *The Way of Love,* trans. Heidi Bostic and Stephen Pluhàcek (London: Continuum, 2002), 6-7.

In "Volume Without Contours," an earlier piece, she writes, "Relations preclude being cut up into units."

✍ Luce Irigaray. *The Way of Love,* trans. Heidi Bostic and Stephen Pluhàcek (London: Continuum, 2002), 7.

This book ends with a fragment: "A Nothingness which is not nothing" (174).

🐝 Bergson, Henri. *Creative Evolution,* trans. Arthur Mitchell (New York: Barnes & Noble, 1907, 1911, 2005), 1.

Even without the book in hand, I recall the power of the first pages. I look them up online, page 1 pops onto my screen, along with some other reader's occasional underlinings and marginal brackets. Through these scanned lines I see the mind at work, the anonymous reader pausing, noting, thinking, and those notes meet my reading, change it.

🐜 Susan Howe. *The Birth-mark: Unsettling the Wilderness in American Literary History* (Middletown: Wesleyan, 1993), 1.

The story by Hawthorne named in this title was a favorite in my youth. Howe is a writer most committed to blurring disciplinary and generic boundaries: a lively interplay of quotes and definitions and photocopies and commentary and poetry, notes begging for the reader's marginalia.

🐞 John Cage. *Silence.* (Hanover: Wesleyan, 1973), 51.

🐌 Edmond Jábes. *The Book of Margins,* trans. Rosmarie Waldrop (Chicago, University of Chicago, 1993), 44.

If there is one writer whose work can send me into reflective revery, it is Jábes, so he sometimes joins me on travels, packed in my bag just in case.

Poem appears in Lee Ann Brown and Leslie Rindoks, eds. *Far From the Centers of Ambition*. (Lorimer Press; Box edition, 2013)

Ecclesiastes (Bible, New Revised Standard Version, 1989)
 In my high school, there was a mural on the wall with the words of the Pete Seeger song "Turn! Turn! Turn! (To Everything There Is a Season)" which means there was also a passage from this book of the Bible on the mural. Then again, it might have been the opening line of Dickens' A Tale of Two Cities. My memory is foggy. And the building in which I attended high school was demolished in 2004.

Richard Feynman. *Six Easy Pieces: Essentials of Physics Explained by Its Most Brilliant Teacher* (New York: Perseus Books, 1994), 117.
 Curious that the publication date falls after the date I thought I'd first read this book. I'm mixing it up with either *Surely You're Joking Mr. Feynman* or perhaps *What Do You Care What Other People Think*, both published in the 1980s.

Martin Heidegger. *Poetry, Language, Thought*, trans. Albert Hofstader (New York: Harper Collins, 1971).
 The verb "to dwell" always conjures Heidegger. We dwell and understand – or, alas, misunderstand.

Albert Einstein. *Relativity: The Special and the General Theory* (New York: Methuen & Co Ltd, 1920), 14.

It's a tidy little book, which is at first surprising.

George Oppen. *Collected Poems* (New York: New Directions, 1975).

I return to this poetic cycle over and over. As did Oppen.

Niels Bohr. *Atomic Physics and Human Knowledge* (Mineola: Dover, 1961, 2010), 9.

For the curious, there is a rough 1957 recording capturing Bohr's voice.

Maurice Merleau-Ponty. *Phenomenology of Perception* trans. Colin Smith (New York: Routledge Classics, 1962, 2008), 455.

When Meena recommended this book, I had little clue how it would hold me – hold me up to think, really. I can barely get through it, distracted by how it provokes my own push to write.

Siri Hustvedt. *A Woman Looking at Men Looking at Women: Essays on Sex, Art, and the Mind* (New York: Simon & Schuster, 2016).

This book collects three earlier volumes in one. It was given to me as a gift, a startling illumination of the loving feeling: *you are paying attention to me.*

Mark E. Kann. *The Gendering of American Politics: Founding*

Mothers, Founding Fathers, and Political Patriarchy (Praeger, 1999).

I read this book in the historic New York Public library building on Bryant Park.

John Stuart Mill. *The Basic Writings of John Stuart Mill: On Liberty, The Subjection of Women and Utilitarianism* (New York: Modern Library, 2002).

Sarah Bakewell. *At The Existentialist Café* (New York: Other, 2016), 7.

I want to judge writers by their writing, yet considering the context of their lives can be important. I vacillate.

Karen Barad. *Meeting the Universe Halfway: Quantum Physics and the Entanglement of Matter and Meaning* (Durham: Duke University Press, 2007).

Some books are worth reading even if I understand only part, understand all the learning and study I have not had, for example, in physics.

This thinking entangles so closely with Rilke, whom I read fiercely at the time, that I must cast a line out to the poem that begins "You who never arrived," translated by Stephen Mitchell (1982). Between this and the poem by Tsvetaeva, a portrait of this writer as a young woman emerges.

✐ Plato, Plato's Republic, Book II.

And Weil, too, discusses the Ring of Gyges, including the observation that "no connexion is formed if thought does not bring it about" (Weil 139).

✐ Fyodor Dostoevsky, *The Brothers Karamazov,* trans. Constance Garnett. (New York: Norton: 1976).

In spite of more recent translations, I read the same version I read in the 1990s, its density part of the pleasure. Even the cover sketch of three heads and a troika link my return to the book with my return to memory of reading it in the past.

✐ Simone Weil. Gravity and Grace, trans. Emma Crawford and Marion von der Ruhr. (New York: Routledge, 1947, 2002).

There is a great deal of recursivity in Weil's writing, the movement of thought. So I , too, return to Weil.

✐ The author's past self could be acknowledged: miscellaneous notebooks

✐ In a chapter entitled "Ontology, Intra-activity, Ethics" in *Meeting the Universe Halfway: Quantum Physics and the Entanglement of Matter and Meaning, Barad writes, "Intra-actions effect what's real and what's possible [...]. And intra-actions effect the rich topology of connective causal relations that are iteratively performed and reconfigured" (393). Each word of many sentences in this book might make for a whole paragraph of discussion, puzzling, and poetry.*

James Baldwin and John Romano. "James Baldwin Writing and Talking." *The New York Times* (New York), Sept. 23, 1979.

Baldwin provokes me to marvel at the power of a single sentence.

Søren Kierkegaard. *Works of Love,* trans. Howard and Edna Hong (New York: Harper, 1962), 27.

Written in 1847, the author calls the collection "Some Christian Deliberations in the Form of Discourses." The *deliberation* seems a useful form of writing.

Albert Einstein. Relativity: *The Special and the General Theory* (New York: Methuen & Co Ltd, 1920), 11.

I cannot finish the book, or not with any sense of achievement, because the figures and equations interfere. Still, the ways numbers, shapes, symbols, and sentences work together to make room for wonder.

Pompei. Maria Sapio, editor. (Naples: Arte'm, 2016).

Not bad for a tourist guide.

Martha Graham. *Blood Memory: An autobiography* (New York: Doubleday, 1991), 17.

Again. The dancer, circling back, creating patterns with the body.

Notes page 138

Muriel Rukeyser, Selected Poems, ed. Adrienne Rich (New York: Library of America, 2004), 123.

The Poem as Mask.

There are many books on Green-Wood Cemetery (Allison Cobb's Green-Wood (2018) and Alexandra Kathryn Mosca's Images of America series edition (2008), for example), but mostly the writing is on the stones themselves, some sinking into the dirt, all silent.

It seems right to end the book at the grave.

Acknowledgements

"**Thread: Riddle of the Physical**" was published in the Studio Lab Showcase of Seisma Magazine in 2020. Seisma Magazine is dedicated to the intersection of art and science.

"A conception is a motion" was published in the anthology *Far from the Centers of Ambition,* edited by Lee Ann Brown and Leslie B. Rindoks, Lorimer Press in 2013.

Thank you to Liesl Schwabe and Abby Paige, who read drafts along the many stages as the shape of this book was emerging, and whose encouragement and discernment helped me find my way out of quite a few writing knots. Loving thanks to John Carimando, for helping get this book as close to my vision as possible, and for listening to me talking through entangling threads every single day. And endless gratitude for the privilege of raising Elsa Souffrant, the brightest light and an inspiration for nearly everything I do, creative and otherwise.

Thank you to Patrick Davis, for the care and vision in bringing this book to the world; it's hard to imagine a better reader. To Peter Campion, my generous and insightful editor. And to Cory Firestine and the whole team at Unbound Edition Press for attention to all the details that make this book a special object.

About the Author

Leah Souffrant is a writer, scholar, artist, and teacher committed to interdisciplinary practice. She is the author of *Plain Burned Things: A Poetics of the Unsayable* (Collection Clinamen, PULG Liège 2017). She has been awarded the New York Foundation for the Arts Fellowship in Poetry and her scholarship was recognized by the Center for the Study of Women & Society. Her poetry has been a finalist for the National Poetry Award. The range of Souffrant's work involves poetics, visual studies and art, translation, and critical work in literature, feminist theory, aesthetics, performance, and the ways knowledge and creative expression are interconnected — across and within writing and other arts. She teaches writing at New York University.

About the Type and Paper

Designed by Malou Verlomme of the Monotype Studio, Macklin is an elegant, high-contrast typeface. It has been designed purposely for more emotional appeal.

The concept for Macklin began with research on historical material from Britain and Europe dating to the beginning of the 19th century, specifically the work of Vincent Figgins. Verlomme pays respect to Figgins's work with Macklin, but pushes the family to a more contemporary place.

This book is printed on natural Rolland Enviro Book stock. The paper is 100 percent post-consumer sustainable fiber content and is FSC-certified.

Entanglements was designed by Eleanor Safe and Joseph Floresca. The Entanglements font was co-created by John Carimando with illustrations by Leah Souffrant..

Unbound Edition Press champions honest, original voices. Committed to the power of writers who explore and illuminate the contemporary human condition, we publish collections of poetry, short fiction, and essays. Our publisher and editorial team aim to identify, develop, and defend authors who create thoughtfully challenging work which may not find a home with mainstream publishers. We are guided by a mission to respect and elevate emerging, under-appreciated, and marginalized authors, with a strong commitment to advancing LGBTQ+ and BIPOC voices. We are honored to make meaningful contributions to the literary arts by publishing their work.

unboundedition.com